A Wall Street Guidebook

for
Journalism and Strategic Communication

About the Author

Alecia Swasy is the Donald W. Reynolds Chair in Business Journalism at Washington & Lee University. Swasy earned her Ph.D. from the University of Missouri after working for more than two decades as an editor and reporter at the *Wall Street Journal, Tampa Bay Times* and other publications.

Swasy is the author of *Soap Opera: The Inside Story of Procter & Gamble* and *Changing Focus: Kodak and the Battle to Save a Great American Company*, both published by Times Books. *How Journalists Use Twitter: The Changing Landscape of U.S. Newsrooms*, based on Swasy's dissertation, was published by Lexington Books.

"*A Wall Street Guidebook* should be essential reading for every aspiring reporter in America. Money is at the heart of almost everything we write about, politics, business, sports, crime and often even love. Alecia Swasy's book is a page turner. She covers the basics of business reporting and so much more thanks to the rare access she had to the country's top business reporters and editors."

—*Susanne Craig, investigative reporter for the* New York Times *and winner of the Pulitzer Prize for coverage of the Trump family's business empire.*

A Wall Street Guidebook

for
Journalism and Strategic Communication

Alecia Swasy

Routledge
Taylor & Francis Group

First published 2020
by Routledge
52 Vanderbilt Avenue, New York, NY 10017

and by Routledge
2 Park Square, Milton Park, Abingdon, Oxon, OX14 4RN

Routledge is an imprint of the Taylor & Francis Group, an informa business

Library of Congress Cataloging-in-Publication Data
Names: Swasy, Alecia, author.
Title: A Wall Street guidebook for journalism and strategic communication / Alecia Swasy.
Description: New York, NY : Routledge, Taylor & Francis Group, 2020. | Includes bibliographical references and index.
Identifiers: LCCN 2020003651 (print) | LCCN 2020003652 (ebook) | ISBN 9780367348038 (hardback) | ISBN 9780367348069 (paperback) | ISBN 9780429328169 (ebook)
Subjects: LCSH: Journalism, Commercial--United States--Guidebooks. | Business communication--United States--Guidebooks. | Communication in management--United States--Guidebooks. | Finance--United States--Sources. | Corporations--United States--Sources.
Classification: LCC PN4784.C7 S93 2020 (print) | LCC PN4784.C7 (ebook) | DDC 070.4/465--dc23
LC record available at https://lccn.loc.gov/2020003651
LC ebook record available at https://lccn.loc.gov/2020003652

ISBN: 978-0-367-34803-8 (hbk)
ISBN: 978-0-367-34806-9 (pbk)
ISBN: 978-0-429-32816-9 (ebk)

Typeset in Arial
by Jennifer Law Young

Visit the eResources: www.routledge.com/9780367348069

Publisher's Note:
This book has been prepared from camera-ready copy provided by the author.

For my mother, Maribel Allison Swasy.

At 99, she's still kicking butts

at the card table.

"If all printers were determined not to print anything till they were sure it would offend nobody, there would be very little printed."

—*Benjamin Franklin, 1731*

CONTENTS

x

Introduction

Wall Street is the $97 trillion epicenter of global capitalism, where the ups and downs of securities trading shape the price of everything from a Starbucks' latte to a Punta Cana winter vacation.

Trouble is, many people don't understand how it's all connected, or how learning financial basics gives them a competitive edge. That's why I wrote this book – to help math-phobic students and young professionals learn the basics of Wall Street so they can be financially-savvy communicators.

A Wall Street Guidebook for Journalism and Strategic Communication is a beginners' guide to demystify financial information and understand how it fits with your future careers. It's written specifically for those two fields because your audiences depend on you to make sense of a complicated world that's intertwined with money.

The guidebook helps you understand financial statements, how companies grow beyond a garage venture to become a public company, how they invest and grow to make a profit and lots more.

Because I sat through a lot of really dull classes (and taught some, too) this book attempts to make sometimes complicated information more palatable. That mission was helped a great deal by the scores of interviews with journalists and corporate communicators, who helped me bring both historical information and current events to life. It helped that many talked about how little they understood Wall Street, finance and accounting when they got their first jobs.

All agreed that context is one of the keys to understanding Wall Street. That's why the book begins with the world's shortest historical account of how

Corporate America, business journalism and corporate communications grew together from America's journey from the farmlands to the factories.

In Chapter One, you'll learn about the titans of industry, including how John D. Rockefeller became one of the first billionaires by ruthless bullying of smaller oil producers. You'll see how early investigative journalists such as Ida Tarbell exhumed the monopolistic maze of Standard Oil, prompting the U.S. Supreme Court to break it into dozens of smaller companies. Rockefeller's damaged reputation helped create the modern-day industry of Public Relations, which has grown into the broader profession of Strategic Communication.

After you read how small ventures led by garage inventors become publicly-traded corporations, you'll learn the various scorecards that Wall Street uses to measure how executives are using shareholders' money. Chapters Two helps demystify key financial statements that public companies must file with the Securities and Exchange Commission, the government watchdog of Wall Street.

Chapter Three shows how some of the new millennium's players, driven by greed and undetected by everyone else, didn't play by the SEC or accounting industry's rules. The cost of their deception was steep – employees and many others lost jobs, homes, small businesses, plus billions of dollars in retirement funds and investments.

Chapter Four goes a bit deeper on financial analysis with key ratios that help you compare companies and perhaps spot potential trouble ahead. And you'll learn about industry-specific metrics on performance, such as how retailers figure out if the cashmere sweaters are best placed in the front or back of the stores.

In Chapter Five, you'll see how the very best journalists use data and documents to hold powerful executives and politicians accountable to the public. For instance, you'll learn how several Pulitzer Prize-winning journalists exhumed stories such as the myth of President Donald Trump's real estate empire and the horrendous tale of motorists killed by oncoming trains because of broken railroad crossing signals.

Strategic Communication professionals explain in Chapter Six about the importance of building trust, one message at a time, in an era where their peers have been tainted by a steady stream of misleading information out of Washington, as well as Wall Street.

Indeed, the rise of social media platforms, such as Twitter, has been a blessing and a curse because one wrong tweet can make or break a client's reputation or brand, and cost the PR person a job. With that in mind, Chapters Seven and Eight address those problems and give tips and guidelines on professional codes of ethics and U.S. securities laws to guide both journalists and PR people.

Today's graduates are entering the communications industry at a time of rapid change. Traditional newspapers have folded their print editions in favor of digital publications run with smaller staffs. Google, Facebook and Amazon have reshaped the digital world by gulping up ad dollars that fueled both news publications and agency commissions.

But the niche for financial information continues to grow for both journalists and PR pros. Legacy media companies such as the *New York Times*, the *Washington Post* and the *Wall Street Journal* have vibrant digital editions supported by subscriptions and advertising revenue. Besides, all three are investing in state-of-the-art technology that speeds up everything from exhuming thousands of pages of government documents to "forensic visual investigations" that recreate news events with satellite photos and eyewitness accounts in war-torn nations.

Chapter Nine tells those stories and introduces readers to start-up media companies that are looking for smart writers who can dig through financial records to give readers even more sophisticated information, from the high-tech future of artificial intelligence and alternative energy, or the food chain basics of corn and chickens.

In closing, Chapter 10 serves up lots of great advice from those who shared their time and talents for this book. We all wish you well in exciting careers that wait ahead. That is, of course, after you finish the book!

Alecia Swasy, Ph.D.
Donald W. Reynolds Chair in Business Journalism
Professor
Washington & Lee University
swasya@wlu.edu

1 | Covering Corporate America

The *Los Angeles Times* hired Marty Baron to cover financial news in 1979, the same year the Federal Reserve deregulated interest rates, a move that triggered angst. "We had double-digit interest rates, double-digit inflation and double-digit unemployment," said Paul Steiger, the *Times* business editor who hired Baron. "It was a scary time." Even cocktail party "chatter among ordinary folk turned to interest rates and investing in real estate."

Steiger figured the 24-year-old Baron could handle almost any story – and would likely beat deadline. One reason: The Lehigh University graduate earned an MBA as well as a Journalism B.A. "Marty was a superstar from the beginning," Steiger said.

A surge in consumer advertising by Fidelity, Vanguard and other mutual funds motivated publishers to create stand-alone sections instead of tucking business news behind sports, in what Steiger called "the boys' section of the paper." The business team doubled to 55 people in five years. Baron was dispatched to New York where he covered the biggest business stories of the 1980s: merger mania, junk bond king Michael Milken of Drexel Burnham Lambert, and Mexico's default on its sovereign debt.

> **"**Business reporting has more impact on people than government. Many people don't realize it. It was our job to help them understand.**"**
> —Marty Baron

"Business news was coming into its own," Baron recalled. "It was fun to be part of a growing" section of the newspaper. "We were shaping and creating a new field in journalism."

At age 29, Baron was named business editor after Steiger left in 1983 to become the *Wall Street*

Journal's economics and markets editor. Baron emphasized reporting that went far beyond quarterly results and stock moves.

> *"Business reporting has more impact on people than government. Many people don't realize it. It was our job to help them understand. The toothpaste you use, the bed you slept in, the car you used to drive to work. Every one of those are produced by private enterprise. The impact on you is far greater than government has in your life. We needed to look at business from the perspective of consumers, investors, communities, employees and, of course, the companies as ongoing enterprises."*

Understanding how Wall Street became such a global force that shapes politics, policies and peoples' lives requires a look back. U.S. capitalism and communications have been intertwined since the Colonial era. News about shipments of sugar or textiles arriving at Eastern seaports expanded to coverage of new stock markets where men haggled over the price of shares of stock to become partial owners of each other's companies. Small exchanges gave way to the New York Stock Exchange. The world's financial capital grew into "Wall Street" named for the 12-foot wooden fence that once circled a 1600s Dutch settlement in lower Manhattan. Runners would carry slips of papers ordering traders on the exchange floor to buy or sell shares in coal, cotton or tobacco companies.

News spread faster in 1867 when Edward A. Calahan reconfigured a telegraph machine to transmit stock prices. (In Europe, Julius Reuters sent stock prices via carrier pigeons to fill in for gaps in telegraph wires.) Thomas Edison gets credit for later improving the device – nicknamed "the ticker" because the machine made a steady ticking noise as it printed prices on narrow strips of paper. By the end of the day, piles of this "ticker tape" sat on the floors of New York investors' offices. The ribbons of paper were tossed out windows for ticker tape parades to honor returning war heroes in the streets below.

The narrow strips of paper required abbreviated stock names, so each company was assigned a ticker symbol. The most-actively traded stocks got a one-letter symbol. American Bell, established after Alexander Graham Bell's invention of the telephone in 1876, had a ticker symbol of "T." Others got two-letters.

Journalists Charles H. Dow and Edward D. Jones founded Dow Jones & Co. in 1882 to publish the Customers' Afternoon Letter for a growing number of consumers turned investors. The two-page newsletter became the *Wall Street*

The Original Stocks of the Dow Jones Industrial Average, 1896

Name	Business	Status of Company
American Cotton Oil Co.	Formed from several mills in Texas and Arkansas to regulate seed prices. Became a corporation in 1889.	Original company remained on DJIA until 1901. Became Best Foods, which is now part of Unilever, the Anglo-Dutch consumer products giant.
American Sugar Co.	Formed in 1891 as sugar refining business.	Now part of ASR Group, a company that combined the Fanjul family's Florida Crystals and Sugar Cane Growers Cooperative of Florida. American Sugar Co. dropped from DJIA in 1930.
American Tobacco Co.	Founded in 1890 and grew from acquisitions of 200 competitors.	U.S. Supreme Court ordered the company to split into parts on grounds of anti-trust violations. Remaining company became Fortune Brands. Dropped from DJIA in 1985.
Chicago Gas Co.	Founded in 1887 and grew from purchase of other Chicago area gas and heating concerns.	Became part of Integrys Energy Group. Chicago Gas was dropped from DJIA in 1915.
General Electric Co.	Formed in 1892 with merger of several electric companies, including one started by Thomas Edison.	Became an aviation, transportation, energy and financial services conglomerate. Financial woes plague what's left of GE, which dropped off DJIA in 2018. It was the last of the original dozen companies to lose its spot on the index.
Distilling & Cattle Feeding Co.	Manufacturer of alcohol.	Sold parts of company to Diageo and American Brands. The rest is now part of Millennium Chemicals, which produces titanium dioxide, an ingredient in paint and sunscreen. Original company lost spot on DJIS in 1899.
Laclede Gas Co.	Supplier of natural gas for street lights and houses.	Renamed Spire Energy, which distributes natural gas in Alabama, Mississippi and Missouri. Dropped off DJIA in 1899.
National Lead Co.	Founded in 1772 in Philadelphia.	Now NL Industries Inc., parent of subsidiaries that sell components such as ball bearing slides and ergonomic computer supports, as well as titanium dioxide pigments. Original National Lead Co. dropped from DJIA in 1916.
North American Co.	Owned utilities and railroads.	In 1946, the company was forced to split up by Securities and Exchange Commission after Congress passed stricter laws to regulate public utilities. North American dropped by DJIA in 1930.
Tennessee Coal, Iron and Railroad Co.	Founded in 1852 with stakes in railroads, coal and iron ore mines.	Merged with competitor U.S. Steel Corp. in 1907. Dropped by DJIA the same year.
U.S. Leather Co.	Founded in New York in 1893. Tanned animal hides to make leather.	The company liquidated in 1952. It was dropped from DJIA in 1928.
U.S. Rubber Co.	Founded in 1892 as tire maker in Connecticut. Also made rubber-soled shoes. The Keds division gets credit for selling first "sneakers" in 1917.	Became Uniroyal Inc., then Uniroyal Goodrich Tire Co. Acquired by Michelin. Dropped from DJIA in 1928.

(*Sources: Business Insider, June 20, 2018, Forbes, July 15, 2011.*)

Journal in 1896. Previously, investors didn't get much factual news coverage on individual companies. That's because company officials could often bribe reporters to write glowing stories to puff up their stock prices. Messrs. Dow and Jones built a reputation for credible, unbiased reporting, which boosted the *Journal's* sales.

The *Journal* editors created the Dow Jones Industrial Average (DJIA) to track daily trading of 12 stocks. The average was just that: the sum of the stocks' closing prices divided by 12.

Over the years, the DJIA, nicknamed "the Dow," grew to 30 companies, and old-timers like coal and tobacco stocks were bumped in favor of newer, more popular stocks.

Business reporting took on a more investigative edge as editors at the turn *1900s* of the 20th century saw the downside of wealthy titans, or "robber barons." Vanderbilt, Rockefeller and Carnegie were gobbling up smaller competitors *"watch* to build monopolies of mines, mills and railroads. They could dictate lower *dog"* commodity prices and wages to become billionaires.

One of the most formidable titans was John D. Rockefeller, who built Standard Oil, largely by driving smaller competitors out of business. Journalist Ida Tarbell persuaded editors at *McClure's* magazine to let her research Rockefeller's empire for a three-part series on the history of Standard Oil.

The project expanded into two years of research for a 12-part series published in 1902 through 1904. Tarbell's work prompted the U.S. Department of Justice to file a lawsuit against Standard Oil. The U.S. Supreme Court ruled that Rockefeller violated anti-trust laws, and Standard Oil was split into 34 separate companies. Tarbell was one of the first "muckrakers" that led to modern day investigative business journalism.

Ironically, Rockefeller's tight-fisted practices also spawned one of the earliest examples of corporate public relations. The oil baron hired a publicist after Tarbell's expose was published, but he quit out of frustration with Rockefeller. That same year, the United Mine Workers were organizing 11,000 miners at Rockefeller's Colorado Fuel & Iron Co., which had refused to increase wages, limit shifts to eight hours or allow workers live outside the company town. Many of the workers' demands were already Colorado law, which managers ignored.

Miners went on strike, prompting Rockefeller to bring in detectives and alert the Colorado governor to send in the National Guard to stifle the uprising. Fires and riots killed 66 men, women and children. News of the deaths spread, confirming Rockefeller's reputation as a ruthless bully in search of greater profits.

To battle the negative news headlines, Rockefeller hired Ivy Lee, who had worked as a reporter covering New York financial news before practicing what would come to be called public relations. Lee is credited with creating the "press release" which gave Pennsylvania Railroad's account of a train accident to journalists before they could interview other sources and witnesses. Lee figured that companies would have a better chance of shaping the coverage if they issued such statements.

His advice to clients: "Tell the truth to journalists because sooner or later the public will find it out anyway." In Rockefeller's case, Lee sent Colorado journalists press releases about coal mine managers' complaints about biased news coverage. Another said it was the union's leaders, not management, who "condoned, if not instigated" violence. He even created fake reports showing the fire that burned the miners' camp was started by a stove. Lee's releases even vilified 82-year-old Mother Jones, the beloved union organizer. (Upton Sinclair, investigative journalist and author of *The Jungle*, named him "Poison Ivy.")

Communications scholars who studied Lee's work found it to be a "dubious" practice because his releases were attributed to mine operators, but were really coming from Rockefeller. Ivy tried to repair Rockefeller's image in later life, sending out photographs of the billionaire handing out dimes to poor kids. His own image will be forever tarnished by the impossible challenge he tackled in the early 1930s. The Nazi party hired Ivy to persuade Americans about "the New Germany."

The Roaring '20s

Americans were in a giddy mood after World War I and went on a spending spree. Retailers peddled easy credit to entice consumers to finance new refrigerators and cars. The economy was shifting to factories. It was the first time that more Americans lived in cities than on farms. Consumer debt doubled from 1920 to 1930.

The tobacco industry was booming, thanks in part to another pioneer of the PR business, Edward Bernays, a nephew of Sigmund Freud. (Communications researchers credit both Ivy and Bernays as either the "founder" or "first true modern practitioner" of PR.) In 1928, young women were encouraged to walk in New York City's Easter Parade while smoking their "torches of freedom" – the liberating nickname for smoking cigarettes in public.

Bernays learned how to spread pro-America messages during World War I as part of the U.S. Committee on Public Information. His uncle's psychology principles shaped his public relations work. Historians note that much of Bernays' success should be credited to his wife, Doris E. Fleischman, who wrote many of the press releases and speeches for her husband's clients.

A graduate of Barnard College, Fleischman worked as a reporter at the *New York Tribune*, and was the first woman to interview Teddy Roosevelt. She wrote often about women of her era, noting the struggles of balancing a career and home life. Indeed, despite all of her work on campaigns, Bernays always met with the clients.

PR campaigns helped stock brokers gain more customers, including women who had previously bought war bonds, but were new to Wall Street investing. It was risky business, considering consumers were encouraged to put down anywhere from 10 to 50 percent of the stock's price and finance the rest "on margin." That meant the buyer could use the actual stocks as collateral.

The buying frenzy sent the DJIA soaring nearly 345 percent from 1923 to 1929. But soon investors reacted to the rising level of debt and too many risky bank loans. Millions bailed and sold their shares. Prices tumbled on October 29, 1929. Investors lost billions in the crash.

The stocks bought on the margin exacerbated the crash because investors couldn't repay their bank loans, causing many financial institutions to fail. The ripple effects hurt all. Businesses closed from bankruptcies, throwing thousands out of jobs. The rock bottom came in 1932. Stocks were worth just 20 percent of the pre-crash highs. About half of U.S. banks failed. Unemployment hit 30 percent with 15 million people out of work.

Thousands lost their homes and were forced to live in flimsy cardboard or tar paper shelters in open fields outside of cities. Some had to dig holes in the ground and cover themselves with cardboard in the rain. Others lived in empty storm pipes.

The camps were called "Hoovervilles" because so many blamed President Herbert Hoover for doing so little to avert the financial crisis or provide relief for its victims. Voters turned on Hoover in the 1932 presidential race, picking Franklin D. Roosevelt, the New York governor who pledged a "new deal for the American people."

FDR pushed for social and corporate reforms in the first-ever "fireside chats" to radio audiences of 60 million listeners. He closed the nation's banks to allow Congress time to pass reforms. The New Deal programs took aim at unemployment by investing in the nation's highways, bridges and expansion of the electric grid. The Public Works Administration and the Tennessee Valley Authority put thousands of men back to work. The TVA brought electricity and radio connections to the rural South.

In banking, FDR pushed for more security for depositers' money with the creation of the Federal Deposit Insurance Corporation (FDIC.) Even if a bank failed, the feds were now telling Americans that they would be reimbursed for losses by the government. He pushed to create the Social Security Administration, to help workers build a nest egg a little at a time from each paycheck.

Creating a Wall Street Watchdog

FDR had much work to do to rein in the stock markets. Before the crash, few in government paid attention to the excesses of Wall Street, figuring it's going up, so why worry?

Congress held hearings to find a solution, which led to the Securities Act of 1933. The Glass-Steagall Act was passed to ban banks from investing consumer deposits in stocks, a practice that led to the financial crisis. Banks had to decide if they would focus on commercial or investment banking. The following year, the Securities Exchange Act of 1934 created the SEC and set laws on "honest dealing," according to sec.gov.

The SEC established guidelines on "publicly-held" companies, which are created when the founder of a private enterprise needs to raise money or "capital" to expand. Instead of borrowing from a bank or relatives, most hire Wall Street advisers or "investment bankers" to put a price tag on the enterprise.

The bankers then find investors to buy shares via an "initial public offering" or IPO. Investors can be other big banks, mutual funds or consumers. The new securities laws were built around a simple notion: If a company wants to sell stock to the public, investors must know what is going on with their money. For the first time, public companies had to have an independent accountant certify that the company's financial statements were accurate.

When the United States declared war on Japan and Germany, U.S. factories converted production of lipstick cases and lingerie to gun cartridges and camouflage netting. In cities like Rochester, N.Y., the biggest employers such as Eastman Kodak Co., General Motors Corp. and Bausch & Lomb suspended a lot of their normal production to supply goods to the troops.

President Roosevelt knew he needed the support of corporate executives to arm, supply and feed the troops in order to win the war. The president backed off his aggressive fight for stricter laws and regulatory agencies. FDR asked corporate titans to lead various commissions or agencies to make them feel included in governing. Productivity and efficiency efforts were embraced by unions and management.

FDR didn't live to see the end of the war. He died in April 1945, just a month before Germany surrendered. His successor Harry S. Truman authorized the use of atomic bombs to end the continued battle with Japan. In August, the bombs were dropped on Hiroshima and Nagasaki. Japan surrendered.

War is hell for those on the front lines, but it proved to be profitable for Wall Street. An analysis of the biggest U.S. companies' stocks, based on market capitalization, showed that stock returns were 17 percent during the war, according to CFA Institute, the national trade group of Certified Financial Analysts. Stocks were also less volatile during the war as compared to peace time. Winning the war helped create a wave of optimism from Wall Street to Main Street.

A surge in consumer spending was fueled by the record number of births between 1946 and 1964, an era dubbed the "Baby Boom." In 1954, U.S. births climbed to four million. By 1965, 40 percent of the population was under the age of 20. Growing families moved to suburbs and planned communities, now reachable via expansive highways.

And they had more time to relax when the Fair Labor Standards Act enforced 40-hour work weeks. To be sure, it was the picture of the middle-class white family, not reflecting the ongoing struggles of African American families or rural poor who didn't have the access to higher education or steady wages. In 1959, about 55 percent of African American families were poor. About one-third of all rural families, especially in the Southern states, lived in poverty.

Part of this gap in household wealth reflected the growing investment in the stock market. The first "share owner census" was done by the New York Stock Exchange in 1952. It showed that only 6.5 million Americans, roughly 4 percent of the population, owned stocks, reflecting the generation's collective memories of the crash of 1929 and the Great Depression that followed. To encourage more Americans to buy shares, the NYSE introduced a monthly investment plan for just $40 a month.

These were boom times for Corporate America. The Dow rose 523 percent from 1949 to 1966, reflecting the prosperous mood, expanding families buying refrigerators for their suburban homes and forming the American middle class.

The "C-suite" in those days consisted of the CEO, or chief executive officer, COO, chief operating officer and CFO, chief financial officer. And it was a very insular club at the very top of Corporate America. The CEOs of a handful of top companies all sat on each other's boards, creating an atmosphere of little oversight of actual business and finance in the old boys' clubs.

Fortune magazine debuted its *Fortune 500* list in July 1955. General Motors was the leading company. The magazine estimated that U.S. companies had about 30,000 execs with incomes of $50,000 or more. The magazine reported that these high-paid execs invested in stocks, bonds and life insurance. The chief owned two cars and "gets along with one or two servants."

Meanwhile, newspapers started to pay more attention to business news, even though budding journalists in the late 1960s and 1970s were more interested in covering the growing social unrest over U.S. military casualties in Vietnam and the civil rights struggle at home.

Allan Sloan recalls applying for jobs covering politics at the *Charlotte Observer* in 1969. Instead, Sloan was assigned to cover business, which he described as the "dregs of journalism."

"You were supposed to fill the space between the stock tables and be nice to people," Sloan said. But he soon showed the impact of good reporting on corporations, breaking news about Duke Power's land purchases and deals with a developer to build apartments that used only electricity vs. natural gas. The costs were passed on to consumers in higher electric bills. Sloan broke the story when Duke was asking state regulators for another rate hike. "It created a whole lot of uproar," he said.

Sloan moved on to bigger papers before moving to *Forbes* magazine. Now he writes a column for *Newsweek* and the *Washington Post*. Instead of following the "be nice to people" advice, Sloan's coverage is often first to cast a skeptical eye on inflated stock prices and questionable business practices. He once characterized it as being the "skunk at the garden party." All evidence to the contrary: His work has earned seven Gerald Loeb Awards, business journalism's highest honor, sometimes called the "Pulitzers for geeks."

Reporters and editors credit several factors for the dramatic improvement in the quality and quantity of business reporting. The first was publishers who saw advertisers buying space in weekly business journals, published by Scripps-Howard and American City Business Journals (ACBJ.) That prompted Knight Ridder to add Business Monday sections to metro papers such as the *Miami Herald* and *Lexington (KY) Herald-Leader*. Another boost to business coverage was Ted Turner's launch of CNN in 1980. News became a 24/7 broadcast so business and other specialized coverage got more air time.

Wall Street coverage on CNN shows hosted by Stuart Varney were popular, prompting the network to add a business show to its Headline News radio. "Listeners wanted to be updated on the stock markets," recalled Lynn Holley, one of the first anchors for the twice-an-hour CNN Radio News business reports. Her coverage started at 6:15 a.m. giving the audience a jump on Asian and European news that would likely influence U.S. markets. "That's where people got hooked," Holley said.

Other networks followed. The Consumer News and Business Channel, a joint venture between NBC and Cablevision, started in 1989, and became CNBC, now owned by Comcast. News Corp. launched Fox Business Network in 2007, promising to be more "business friendly" than CNBC.

Coverage of Wall Street and giant corporations exploded as the nation's political climate shifted from the more liberal 1970s to a conservative, pro-business tenor set by President Ronald Reagan. He had campaigned on a platform of cutting taxes and blamed the nation's ills on a bloated federal government. He promised to cut regulations and taxes.

Reagan's cabinet drew many leaders from Wall Street, including Donald Regan, former CEO of the Merrill Lynch securities firm, who was his treasury secretary and later chief of staff. He and others pushed for deregulation of banking and securities.

Commercial banks in the business of basic consumer checking and savings accounts wanted Glass-Steagall to be repealed so they could get into the more lucrative business of investing in stocks and bonds. Meanwhile, the savings and loan associations, nicknamed "S&Ls" or "thrifts," wanted to diversify.

Thrifts were even the heroes in classic films like "It's a Wonderful Life." George Bailey, played by the lovable Jimmy Stewart, gave up his college money and dream to see the world to stay home and run the Bailey Building and Loan. Without George Bailey, working-class families would've been trapped in the banker-slumlord Mr. Potter's crummy rental properties.

In real small towns, about 4,000 S&Ls held half of the nation's mortgages by 1980. They operated under strict federal rules on interest rates paid for deposits and mortgage lending. S&Ls adhered to requirements on down payments, credit checks and appraisals. But the deregulation push brought relaxed rules. In 1982, Congress passed the Garn-St. Germain Depository Institutions Act, which the president hailed as "the most important legislation for financial institutions in the last 50 years."

Meanwhile, on Wall Street, a man named Lew Ranieri at Salomon Brothers came up with an idea to make more money: collateralized mortgage obligations or CMOs. This was a repackaging of mortgages into securities that could be resold to investors. This created the mortgage-backed securities market.

"This was a huge source of new money for Wall Street," said Robert Trigaux, who was Washington Bureau Chief of the *American Banker* from 1983 until 1991. By selling their mortgages to Salomon and others, the S&Ls and banks had "fresh money to lend anew," he said.

The relaxed laws also allowed S&Ls to make riskier loans to commercial real estate developers. And thrifts loosened their standards on home mortgages, such as no down payment and a loan of 100 or even 120 percent of the appraised value of the house.

"Back then, the idea of a home losing significant value was almost unheard of,"

Trigaux said. "More unsavory S&Ls doctored their appraisals to fit their profit needs when all else failed. Many thrifts died simply from the mismatch of paying lots for deposits but making lower interest rate mortgages. That does not work."

One of the more infamous S&L villains was Charles H. Keating Jr., who defrauded Lincoln Savings & Loan Association while chairman of the Irvine, Ca. thrift. Keating used depositors' money to invest into land deals that turned out to be completely bogus. Meanwhile, Keating used the S&L as his "personal cash machine," according to the *New York Times*, pocketing $34 million for himself and another $1.3 million for political contributions.

Lincoln had unreported losses of $135 million. Keating hired a consultant and lobbyist named Alan Greenspan, who helped him find buddies in Congress to persuade banking regulators to loosen the rules.

The group was dubbed the "Keating Five" and included Senators John McCain and John Glenn. Reporters once asked Keating if his payments to politicians worked. His response: "I want to say in the most forceful way I can: I certainly hope so."

The senators were investigated by the Senate Ethics Committee, which questioned their actions and the campaign donations of $1.5 million from Keating. Only one of the five got a formal reprimand from the committee.

Lincoln ranked as one of the biggest failed thrifts among the more than 1,000 S&Ls that collapsed between 1986 and 1995. Keating was convicted of fraud, racketeering and conspiracy in state and federal courts, but the verdicts were later overturned. He served just four and a half years in prison.

As a result of the thrift crisis, real estate markets collapsed, and taxpayers had to bail out the mess. The federal Resolution Trust Corp. was created to liquidate all the foreclosed houses and commercial properties across the country. Taxpayers picked up the tab for the $130 billion failure. "It truly was a debacle, layered upon debacle of bad leadership in Washington, Wall Street and the financial industry in general," Trigaux said.

As for consultant and lobbyist Greenspan, he went on to become Federal Reserve chairman, earning high praise for his adept handling of monetary policy in the late 1980s and early 1990s. Greenspan was treated like a deity, but Americans would soon realize even the Fed chairman can make some really bad calls.

An Enduring Case in Communication Under Fire

In September, 1982, U.S. consumers were rattled about the safety of over-the-counter pain killers after news broke that seven people died after taking cyanide-laced Extra-Strength Tylenol capsules. Johnson & Johnson, the maker of Tylenol, had to scramble its public relations and advertising teams to handle a growing crisis. Tylenol was used by more than 100 million consumers and produced 19 percent of J&J's profits in 1982.

J&J first learned of the problem when a Chicago reporter called for comment after the city's medical examiner announced that people were dying from ingesting the tainted pills. The company reacted quickly and launched an aggressive campaign via news reporters and ads to tell consumers to stop using the product.

All advertising and production of Tylenol was suspended and all products in the Chicago area were removed from store shelves. When two more bottles were found to be tainted, the company recalled all Tylenol products across the nation. In just over two months, J&J designed a tamper-resistant package of Tylenol to get the product back on store shelves.

The decisive moves were lauded by all because it showed the company made the right calls for the right reasons. Its first priority was to keep consumers safe, and the company didn't flinch about media coverage. Instead, executives held press briefings and updates. CEO James Burke went on "60 Minutes" and other national television shows to address the issue. Experts call it the "Forgiveness and Sympathy strategy" because it wins over the public by accepting responsibility for the problem.

The genius behind the campaign was Larry Foster, a Journalism grad from Penn State who worked as a night editor at the *Newark News* before joining J&J to build its first public relations department in the late 1950s, and eventually became a vice president. He pushed for the fast, candid response to the crisis, including CEO Burke's many TV appearances.

"Johnson & Johnson's reputation and credibility were at stake, as was the compelling need to protect the public," Foster wrote in *Robert Wood Johnson – The Gentleman Rebel*, his biography of the company patriarch.

Foster, who died in 2013, was named by PR Week one of the ten most influential public relations executives of the 20th century. Indeed, the J&J Tylenol case study is still the gold standard in crisis communication studies.

The 1980s also sealed Reagan's reputation as a brilliant political communicator. But he didn't win any praise from the working poor, minorities or union members. One of the greatest setbacks to economic prosperity for the middle and working class Americans was Reagan's tough stance with striking Air Traffic Control Workers in 1981. About 13,000 members of the Professional Air Traffic Controllers Association went on strike after failed talks with the Federal Aviation Administration to raise their pay and shorten their work weeks. Thousands of flights were canceled. Two days into the strike, Reagan axed more than 11,000 controllers.

Reagan, who once bragged how he was the first president of the Screen Actors' Guild to lead a strike, changed all future labor-management bargaining. "Reagan's unprecedented dismissal of skilled strikers encouraged private employers to do likewise," said Joseph A. McCartin, a labor historian at Georgetown University.

Union membership continued to drop as manufacturers shifted production to foreign countries. Meanwhile, the U.S. dollar's value dropped against the Japanese yen, prompting Honda and others to build cars in the heart of America's Rust Belt. Honda was the first Japanese automaker to build a U.S. factory, dubbed "transplants," in Marysville, Ohio in 1982. Nissan followed with a Smyrna, Tenn. plant in 1983. Toyota was next with its Camry plant in Georgetown, Kentucky.

GM and other U.S. automakers were hit hard because the transplant factories were largely non-union shops and could build a car for about $500 to $800 less than U.S. automakers. The "Big Three" automakers' share of the U.S. auto sales dropped from 84 percent in the late 1970s to 69 percent in the late 1980s.

The U.S. automakers were feeling the full brunt of their failure to respond fast enough to the growing appetite for more fuel-efficient imported cars after the oil crises of the 1970s. Other U.S. companies that had behaved as near monopolies for decades were in similar stages of denial about foreign competition.

Let the Good Times Roll!

Consumers showed little interest in cutting their own spending, thanks to the credit-card lifestyle of the 1980s, which sociologists dubbed "conspicuous consumption." The "yuppies" – the acronym for "young upwardly mobile professionals" – took on huge mortgages to buy grand five-bedroom houses with three-car garages. The "McMansions" replaced their parents' generation of modest brick ranch homes from the 1950s.

And their typewriters collected dust in the closet after a Harvard dropout named Bill Gates and his buddy Paul Allen, founded Microsoft and the age of personal computers, or PCs. Competitors popped up quickly. Apple Inc. introduced the Macintosh personal computer in 1984 at a price of $2,495. Four months later, Apple had sold 70,000 Macs.

The internet started to attract consumers when what would later become known as AOL launched its online service in 1985. Microsoft reshaped the world of computing with its consumer-friendly Windows operating system, which provided even newbies an easy-to-use gateway into producing its Word documents, Excel spreadsheets and much more.

The company went public in 1986 at $21 a share. And the 31-year-old Gates became the world's youngest billionaire. All of the high-tech growth was a boom for Wall Street, which enjoyed a five-year bull market. It fueled the growth of a smaller stock exchange, the Nasdaq, which attracted such newcomers as Microsoft and Apple.

In 1988, the *Wall Street Journal* expanded to three sections to expand its investing and marketing coverage. The paper was thick with Tiffanys and Barneys ads. Dozens of "tombstone ads" – nicknamed for their simplistic bare bones type in square boxes – filled the pages. The ads were placed by investment banks to congratulate themselves for doing their jobs advising clients on mergers or stock offerings.

Ellen Pollock was hired to help edit the *Journal's* new legal coverage in 1989. "We had money to travel to find the stories. Breaking news was important, but we wanted to find the stories behind the stories."

James Stewart became the *Journal's* page-one editor, who acts as gate keeper of the front page's columns one, four and six. Column one was home to corporate investigative pieces or narratives about rural poverty, while four was home to lighter features. Column six was the place for "DBIs," dull but important stories, such as the inevitable story on the rise or fall of copper prices.

Reporters often took months to dig into investigative projects, such as Walt Bogdanich's reporting on faulty lab tests for cervical cancer. He found overworked and underpaid technicians testing pap smear slides in labs. Other technicians analyzed the slides at home instead of labs.

These "pap mills" raced to do hundreds of slide screenings. The result: the labs missed signs of cervical cancer in 20 to 40 percent of the tests. His series of stories, which earned the Pulitzer Prize, led to tougher laws to ensure accuracy, such as proficiency testing for technicians and regulation on labs.

By 1987, there were economic signs of a coming market correction. The U.S. trade deficit was bigger than expected and the dollar dropped against other currencies. The Federal Reserve, led by the new chairman Greenspan, raised interest rates. Besides, the run-up in stock prices leading up to the fall of 1987 showed the market was overheated.

On October 19, 1987, the DJIA plummeted 22.6 percent, earning it the nickname of "Black Monday." The 508-point plummet was the biggest crash ever. The *New York Times* headline read: "Does 1987 Equal 1929?"

"What it did signify was the beginning of the destruction of markets by dumb computers," wrote Floyd Norris, reporter for the *Times'* Business section. "Or, to be fair to the computers, by computers programmed by fallible people and trusted by people who did not understand the computer programs' limitations. As computers came in, human judgment went out."

The drop was fueled by computerized trading of stocks and new investments that gave traders greater hedges against risk. "Portfolio insurance" used "stock index futures" and "options" to give big institutional investors a soft landing in case of a declining market. Here's how it worked: The portfolio insurance protected the traders by kicking in more sales of futures contracts, which lock in prices based on future value of stocks that make up the DJIA or S&P 500.

When the market began to drop, computer programs automatically sold index futures. That meant buyers of the futures wanted lower prices and sold the actual stocks. The combination tanked the market and set off a panic. And it spread around the globe. The next day, the New York Stock Exchange halted trading in many stocks. And the Chicago Mercantile Exchange threatened to halt trading in stock index futures.

Norris recalled how Goldman Sachs and Salomon Brothers, two top brokerages, agreed to make a move to stop the losses. Their traders put in buy orders to reopen any stock in the S&P 500. It worked and prices recovered, Norris said.

Unlike past market drops, the 1987 crash didn't reflect a banking crisis and it didn't lead to a recession. Indeed, the Dow regained half of its losses in just two days. These were the earliest days of computerized trading, versus its dominance in current stock trading. The crash brought reforms including "circuit breakers" that halt trading if stocks dive too quickly.

Mergers and acquisitions made headlines as big companies looked for ways to finance even bigger deals. Another financial instrument that became popular was the "leveraged buyout" or LBO. A leveraged buyout means the acquiring company borrows a lot of money, also known as "leverage" to do the deal. The buyer often uses the target company's assets as collateral for loans.

The strategy in LBOs is to buy back the public's shares and take the company private. The new management slashes costs to make it pretty with profits. When the market looks inviting, the owners do a new public offering to sell shares and recoup the investment and pay off the debt.

Some experts consider LBOs to be cold-blooded deals because they are generally unwelcome bidders and load up the combined companies with bonds rated below investment grade quality, or "junk" bonds.

Mega deals like Kohlberg Kravis Roberts & Co.'s takeover of R. J. Reynolds' for $26.4 billion in 1989 marked the largest LBO in history. The battle for the company pitted top investment bankers against each other, ratcheting up the final price tag to $109 a share, up dramatically from about $55 a share trading price seen before the deal. And true to LBOs, the deal relied heavily on debt to take the company private. Just three years later, the company once again sold stock to go public. But the RJR deal ended up as a crummy investment for KKR. The company did go public again, with initial investor enthusiasm. As the share price dropped, KKR ended up trading its stake in RJR in another deal for Borden Inc. RJR was eventually sold off in pieces.

Central characters such as F. Ross Johnson, CEO of RJR Nabisco, became the subject of page-one narratives in the *Journal*. Johnson was once described as having a big mouth and even bigger tastes in perks, such as a fleet of 10 airplanes so he could jet about with golfer Jack Nicklaus, among others.

And there were villains, such as financier Michael Milken who built Drexel Burnham Lambert's junk bond business. When that market tanked, the company was liquidated. Massive layoffs swept Wall Street firms. Milken served 22 months in prison for illegal trades to boost profits.

The *New York Times* expanded its business coverage with a hefty Sunday section with long narratives, personal finance coverage and reviews of top-selling business books on corporate takeover dramas such as *Barbarians at the Gate: The Fall of RJR Nabisco*. Stewart from the *Journal* wrote a best-selling book *Den of Thieves* about the downfall of Milken and others.

Baron, the Wall Street reporter for the *Los Angeles Times*, remembers the arrogance and money mania of the time:

> *"Even junior analysts were making a fortune. I recall one analyst comparing his job to mine as a reporter covering Wall Street and major corporations: 'You and I do pretty much the same thing. The difference is I make more money at it than you do.' He wasn't really wrong, although I was examining business through a wider societal lens and he was strictly looking at profitability and growth. Confronted with New York's oppressively high costs – living in a one-bedroom, ground-level apartment in Brooklyn – I finally felt compelled to ask for a raise. I was placated with $25 a week extra, the sort of acquiescence that was laughable on Wall Street."*

Which IPO raised the biggest pile of loot on opening day? Who is the richest CEO?

Wall Street loves to keep such scores, almost as much as Major League Baseball.

Learning how investors, analysts and auditors interpret the scorecards helps you break news, and spot trends and potential problems. In turn, you'll write smarter stories, press releases or marketing pitches that better inform the public, consumers and other stakeholders.

Let's start with a very basic question: How does a company make money? The easiest way to understand is to look at a ubiquitous company like McDonald's. The fast-food giant generates sales, also called revenue, from consumers buying burgers, fries or nuggets.

After the company pays its employees, suppliers, taxes and other expenses, the money that's left over is net income, also called earnings or profits.

Any company that is publicly-held must release quarterly financial reports to the Securities and Exchange Commission and to the public. The companies are required to file the financials within 35 days after the end of the quarter, and 60 days after the end of the year.

Companies can choose to follow a calendar year as its "fiscal year" or it can pick another 12-month period, such as July to June, if its business cycle justifies a different time frame. For instance, retailers might choose December 31 as the year-end date to capture the important holiday sales. But others figure that date is too soon after the most hectic season, so the fiscal-year ends January 31.

Journalists' first glimpse of the quarterly results is the corporate press release. Companies tend to issue the press release via paid services such as BusinessWire or PR Newswire, or send them directly to financial news wires such as Bloomberg News, Dow Jones News Wire or Reuters, the big three of real-time news. Most companies also post the report on their websites.

The press release is a boiled-down version of the official quarterly SEC filing known as the "10-Q" which is usually filed at a later date. The annual version of the entire year is called the "10-K."

There are all sorts of other SEC filings, all using a number and a letter, such as the "8-K," which is used to report anything that is considered "material," meaning it could impact the company's current or future financial health. The company must file that within four days of the event.

For instance, the company files an 8-K when it issues the earnings press release, and then follows up with the 10-Q. Other events that would require an 8-K: selling a division or if the CEO quits.

The actual 10-Q includes four key documents: The Income Statement, Balance Sheet, Cash Flow and Stockholders' Equity statement. The 10-Q is especially vital when a company doesn't include all of the financial statements in the press release. Small companies, for instance, tend to put just the income statement and balance sheet in the press releases.

The SEC's website (sec.gov) offers guides on reading the financial statements, which it labels as easy to read as baseball box scores. But that assumes we're all baseball fans. So, let's dissect the reports from top to bottom.

Statement of Income

This shows three months and year-to-date results. For most companies, the "top line" income statement figure is revenue or sales, which is the goods or services provided and booked during that period. Journalists tend to use the terms "sales" and "revenue" interchangeably. Make sure it's the "total revenue or sales" because some companies break sales or revenue into separate lines for different operations.

To understand each of these statements, it's helpful to locate a recent 10-Q to study as you learn about each part:

- *Go to SEC.GOV.*

- *Click on FILINGS tab, which takes you to FILINGS & FORMS page.*

- *Click on SEARCH FOR FILINGS.*

- *Next, you enter a company name or its ticker symbol. Let's use Walmart or ticker symbol WMT. Sometimes, there will be multiple options listed. You want Walmart Inc.*

- *To the left of the corporate name is a CIK number, a 10-digit number assigned to any company filing with the SEC.*

- *If you click on that number, you're now at the latest company filings.*

- *Find the 10-Q in the list.*

- *A click on DOCUMENTS button takes you to the filing and various exhibits.*

- *Click on highlighted WMTFORM 10-Q item, and you're finally at the actual SEC filing.*

Think of that total as the big pot of money that gets smaller as companies deduct all the costs related to running a business, such as administrative or operating expenses.

Next, the company has to report interest paid or earned, then income taxes. This takes you to the "bottom line" of the income statement – net income. Net income is reported as both a full-dollar amount, usually in millions or billions, depending on the size of the company. Then as "earnings per share" or EPS, which are calculated by dividing that full-dollar net income number by the number of shares "outstanding" or issued to shareholders.

Bloomberg and other news organizations use the "diluted earnings per share" figures vs. EPS because it more accurately reflects the dilutive effect of issuing more shares, such as when employee stock options are converted to shares.

Now, first-time readers of financial statements see earnings per share might think: "Wow, so if Bubbly Biz Inc. earned $1.50 a share, and I owned 100 shares, I'd get a check for $150!"

Sorry, but the EPS figure is just one way to compare companies to each other. The net income isn't divvied up among holders; the money is re-invested back into the business.

To be sure, some companies do share profits with stockholders via a "dividend." These can be paid quarterly, while others pay them twice a year. Companies that need to reinvest every dime of profits into growing the business usually don't pay a dividend.

When studying these key measures, it's essential to compare the latest quarterly results to the comparable year-earlier quarter. That provides a true "apples-to-apples" comparison which is the fairest way to judge the results. There are exceptions to this rule, such as banking, where it's more appropriate to look at performance by sequential quarters instead of year-over-year comparisons.

For some companies, such as H&R Block, most of its sales and income come from the months leading up to the April 15 federal tax filing deadline. Or, for retailers, a chunk of sales and income depend on the crucial holiday season between Thanksgiving and Christmas.

News organizations weigh a variety of factors when deciding if there's an actual story to be written from quarterly results. The first newsroom transmission to subscribers at Bloomberg and Dow Jones, for instance, is via automated programs, reviewed by journalists, who then send out key numbers. Stories that follow are kept rather short, unless news warrants a longer explanation.

One reason is the results are widely-anticipated because most companies brief Wall Street analysts prior to the actual release. The analysts then write reports that are circulated to clients and media.

Services such as Bloomberg, Reuters, Zacks Investment Research, and Yahoo! Finance are a quick way to find the "consensus" earnings and sales estimate based on the average of analysts' predictions. When the actual numbers come out, they're reported as having "beat, met or missed" the estimates. In some cases, the company's release of results can be truly revealing because analysts don't bother with forecasts on smaller companies.

Some investors pay little attention to the "beat" or "missed" labels given that the numbers have been telegraphed in advance. Indeed, it's not often that a company actually misses the consensus number. S&P Global Market

Intelligence reported that two-thirds of the companies on the S&P 500 report earnings that are higher than the street's estimates.

Regardless, the estimates have been factored into the company's stock price going into the day of the public release of results. If a company surpasses the EPS prediction by a large amount, its shares could rise. On the other hand, markets can be brutal on misses. McKinsey consultants recall one quarter when eBay missed its fourth-quarter consensus estimate by a penny and its share price tanked 22 percent.

When journalists write earnings stories, they tend to include four essentials from the results.

1. Sales or revenue – most reporters just use the same term used on the press releases.

2. Net income in full-dollar figure.

3. Net income per fully-diluted share.

4. The year-earlier figures to compare to the latest sales, net income and per-share results.

The story usually includes whether the company met, beat or missed analysts' predictions.

Naturally, there are other things to watch for in the income statement or press release. They include:

- Look at the top of the income statement and you'll usually see that figures are abbreviations of millions or billions for the biggest companies. For instance, the table might list net income as $34.6. But remember that's in billions, so it's really $34,600,000,000. Zeros and decimal places can be accidentally deleted in editing, so standard style is to write it as: $34.6 billion.

- The exception is the earnings per share figure which is in dollars and cents, say, $2.95.

- Always look at the number of shares outstanding in the most recent quarter vs. the same quarter last year. If the company had a stock buyback program in the course of the year, you'll see change in the number of shares outstanding. That, in turn, puffs up the per-share figure because the total shares outstanding is the denominator in calculating the earnings per share. (Total net income/shares outstanding = EPS.)

- Watch for footnotes labeled (a), (b), etc. Or (1), (2), etc. This is where the company discloses any special charges, such as legal settlements or environmental fines, that decreased the quarter's results. Or special, or one-time gains, such as proceeds from the sale of a division, tax credits, settlement of a lawsuit, favorable currency conversions, that boost the results. Footnotes can be in the current or year-earlier quarter. When writing the story, just make sure to add a line explaining that the most-recent quarter (or year-earlier one) reflected a charge or gain of whatever amount from whatever happened.

- Some companies present the results in side-by-side columns listed as:

Q3 '20	Q3 '19

That simplifies the comparison because the current number can be quickly compared to the year-earlier result. Beware of press releases that present the results in sequential order like this:

Q3 '20	Q2 '20	Q1 '20	Q4 '19	Q3 '19

The accurate comparison in this listing is to compare the first column to fifth one, Q3-2020 vs. Q-3-2019.

Balance Sheet: A Ledger of Assets vs. Liabilities

Let's move on to the second financial statement.

The Balance Sheet, which is a snapshot in time of the company's assets (real estate, factories, inventory, cash, securities or anything of value) as compared to its liabilities (anything owed to others, such as loans, payroll or taxes). It also shows Shareholders' or Stockholders' Equity, which is the owners' claims on the company.

The Balance Sheet is a snapshot of the company's financial health at that point in time, such as the end of the quarter listed on the document. The numbers are always changing just as your bank balance goes up or down as you deposit your paycheck or make a car payment.

This statement shows the balance of what a company owns minus what it owes. Assets are what a company owns, such as actual property, equipment, cars, trucks and any inventory, such as a retailer's warehouse of Christmas bikes that have yet to be shipped to the stores. Assets can also include any cash.

The flipside of the equation is a company's "liabilities" or any money that it owes, such as loans, mortgages, upcoming wages, insurance, legal fees or taxes.

The third component of a Balance Sheet is "shareholders' equity" or the owners' claims on the company. Shareholders' equity shows how the company raised capital to sustain the business, such as how much owners invested to buy the shares, among other things.

Statement of Cash Flows

The Statement of Cash Flows, uses information from other statements to show three measures of performance: cash from operations, cash from investing and cash from financing activities.

The most important part of this statement is cash flow from operations. Basically, is the company churning cash from its core business, such as sales of chicken nuggets? If this isn't a positive number, that could mean trouble because companies are eventually supposed to generate cash from everyday operations.

Cash from investing includes money invested in physical property via capital expenditures. It can also include any proceeds from the sale of securities held in the company's investment portfolio.

Finally, the statement shows cash from financing, such as dividends, share buybacks, proceeds from the sale of more shares, bonds or loans from banks.

Cash from investing can be a negative number and be considered a healthy sign. That's because the company is investing in growth. For instance, Exxon and other oil companies must invest a lot of money in updating pipelines, refineries and other parts needed to turn oil into gasoline. But it throws off billions in cash from operations each quarter so it has plenty of cushion to cover that investment in improvements and expansion.

After you've reviewed each of these sections of the financial statements, look up the news stories that were written after the company issued the press release and filed the 10-Q.

For instance, most news organizations write a full-blown story on WMT's earnings, given its dominance in groceries and merchandise sales. Plus, its battle with Amazon for e-commerce shoppers is an ongoing issue for the survival of "bricks-and-mortar" retailers.

Check CNBC.com or Yahoo! Finance for the "quick hit" stories. For a deeper analysis of the results, it's best to look up the coverage in the New York Times, Wall Street Journal or on Bloomberg News.

Any journalist or strategic communicator knows the Wall Street Journal is a must-read for daily coverage and deeper dives into a company, its competitors and the global forces that impact its businesses as well as the broader economy. The Journal also provides a rich database of past and current information on a company.

Subscribers can go to quotes/wsj.com to get real-time stock prices, as well as benchmarks like the stock's 52-week high and low prices and current share prices for its competitors. The site also gives you access to press releases, stories by the Journal and its sister publications Barron's, Dow Jones Newswires and MarketWatch.

For larger companies and those working on Wall Street, another must-have is a Bloomberg terminal, which is a gateway to all sorts of financial data and news. It also features Bloomberg Intelligence, the company's own team of analysts and their research reports.

Bloomberg also gives you access to other news sources, data on commodities, credit and bond markets. For students, you might be lucky enough to attend a university that has access to the Bloomberg terminal, thanks to the company's generosity to some business journalism programs. Many business schools buy access for their students. For those on Wall Street, it's a pricey subscription: $24,000 a year.

"The Bloomberg"

Matt Winkler, a bond reporter in the *Journal's* London bureau, met a Merrill Lynch trader who seemed to have better market insights on bond pricing. The trader explained that he got real-time and historical comparisons data from a new source called "the Bloomberg." Merrill Lynch was the first company to get 22 of the beige desktop boxes that provided information such as the value of debt instruments based on the bond's yield and price history. The terminal was created by a former Salomon Brothers general partner Michael Bloomberg.

Winkler was "instantly captivated by what Bloomberg was doing" but realized it was a threat to Dow Jones' growing stake in Telerate, which provided real-time data to clients. That acquisition cost Dow Jones $1.5 billion. Bloomberg was, indeed, a growing threat. The service had 5,000 subscribers by 1986.

When he returned to the states in 1987, Winkler and a Journal colleague decided to write a page-one story about Bloomberg and its potential to create chaos in the growing niche of electronic market data. The terminal was a threat to media companies like Dow Jones, Telerate and Reuters, as Bloomberg attracted more big-name clients, including the World Bank. Even the Vatican had one in its funds' management office.

While reporting the story, Winkler got to know Mike Bloomberg, who called about a year later asking him for advice over a miso soup and sushi lunch. The entrepreneur wanted to know what it would take to add original news to the terminal's offerings.

Winkler laid out a scenario to test whether this newbie to news would have the chops to dive into the news business. What happens when reporters write tough stories about his own clients? Was the CEO prepared for their ultimatum: Kill the story or lose their subscriptions to the Bloomberg terminals?

Bloomberg assured Winkler that he wouldn't flinch on news content even if it irked his clients. "Our lawyers will love the fees you generate," he told Winkler.

And he persuaded Winkler to join as his first employee and editor in chief in 1990. He recruited a team of journalists to staff Bloomberg News. The early days brought plenty of challenges, such as lack of name recognition when they called Wall Street contacts. Winkler recalled how they were told: "We don't need any stationery so stop calling" because they were confused with a Wall Street letterhead printer called Blumberg," Winkler said.

Doubtful that anyone still makes that mistake. Bloomberg's first 22 terminals grew to more than 330,000 worldwide. As of late 2019, Bloomberg News had about 2,700 journalists and analysts in 120 countries.

The Quarterly Financial Press Release

The SEC passed Regulation Fair Disclosure, or Reg FD, in 2000 to combat the practice of companies disclosing key information to a small group of investors or analysts before releasing it to the rest of the world.

That special preview often meant a lucky few got warnings about earnings, and could possibly profit from an unfair access to non-public information. It also looked a lot like insider trading, when investors use confidential information to play the market. And that's illegal.

The SEC also granted the public access to listen during CEO conference calls with Wall Street analysts. This is one of the few times when the CEO or CFO fields questions that dig deeper into the financial statements. To be sure, the public and press still can't ask questions during the call.

Any additional information is welcomed because the company-issued news release is often as clear as mud. Unlike the 10-Q, corporate communications and investor relations managers can choose which numbers to highlight on the first pages of the press release. Naturally, it's in the company's best interest to put the sunniest spin on the results, hoping to shape the press coverage and public perception of the company.

For instance, the press release will often highlight non-GAAP (Generally Accepted Accounting Practices) numbers first. That's legal, as long as the company uses GAAP numbers in the actual financial statements. And the SEC requires that company's give equal or more space to GAAP figures.

An example of this is a company using "adjusted" earnings per share (EPS) figures instead of fully-diluted EPS. As you learned earlier, the latter is the most accurate per-share number because it reflects all shares outstanding and any securities that can be converted to common shares. The adjusted EPS, however, uses EBITDA – earnings before interest expense, income taxes, depreciation and amortization. That's a lot of adjusting!

Think of it this way: adjusted figures are comparable to you counting your pay as if that FICA chunk wasn't deducted. Or paying your mortgage without any interest charges. It's not an accurate portrayal of the numbers.

"Earnings releases today are often indecipherable," said Chet Wade, retired vice president of corporate communications for Dominion Energy. But EBITDA numbers are what Wall Street analysts want to see in order to evaluate the underlying operations of a company.

"Analysts are very forgiving of one-time charges," Wade said. "But those charges are real dollars that affect the balance sheet and your ability to do business." It's important to remember that analysts are "all about tomorrow" and how everything will affect the next quarter. "The earnings release is a historical document."

The press release includes a narrative section quoting the company's CEO. This is where most offer the self-congratulatory quotes about delivering "outstanding results that reflect our focus on products and strategic opportunities."

To be sure, some news organizations will actually publish such quotes, especially in early versions of the web story before the reporter gets more detail from the conference call with Wall Street analysts.

It's important to remember that reporters want quotes that enrich the reader's understanding of the underlying fundamentals of the company. Business journalists must provide a deeper analysis that includes: What parts of the company's business or geographic markets are growing or struggling? How is the company faring versus competitors? What global forces – such as currencies, lower oil prices or political unrest – are helping or hurting the performance?

Frankly, a CEO is paid millions plus stock options and bonuses to do his job. Atta-boy quotes from the CEO are akin to a reporter praising herself for filing a story by deadline. *It's the least that is expected!*

Earnings Story Template

Earnings stories should be kept short because they reflect historical information from the previous quarter. Here's a template you can follow to write a story from a company's quarterly-earnings release.

_____(Insert company name including Co., Inc. or Corp.) posted/reported higher/lower/improved/strong/weaker first/second/third/fourth quarter earnings/results, reflecting/_____(what was the biggest issue that hurt/helped the company results?

If the company gives a forecast for upcoming results, put it in the second or third paragraph, because that is forward-looking news. Now, get back to the results.

The _____(insert boiler plate on what the company does. i.e. Cincinnati-based consumer products maker, largest North American auto company, a leading Internet provider, etc.) said net income/profit was *$full dollar amount*, or *$xx.xx a share*, up/down xx% from *$full dollar amount*, or *$xx.xx a share*, in the year-earlier quarter.

NOTE: If the current or year-earlier figure included a special gain/charge (such as discontinued operations, acquisition, etc.) note it and say the exact amount it added/subtracted from the net per-share figure.

Revenue/Sales (*use the term the company uses*) rose/ticked up/fell/dropped *xx percent* to *$full-dollar figure*, compared with/up/down from *$full-dollar amount* in the year-earlier period/quarter.

Tell us what analysts expected.

Analysts polled by Thomas Reuters/whatever service/investment firm who did the survey projected earnings of *$x.xx per-share figure* on revenue of *$xxx.*

Then break it down to show what strengths/weaknesses contributed to the results. For instance, did a certain division/brand/geographic region do well? Or is one dragging down the results.

Put in some industry context: what are competitors experiencing? i.e. If you're covering Coke, add some perspective on Pepsi's results, trends in the beverage industry.

Put in any other news the company announces, which is common in an earnings report, i.e. declaration of a dividend. If the company boosts/cuts its dividend, that's bigger news that needs to be in the second or third paragraph.

3 | A Few Bumps – and Crashes on the Digital Highway

Tracy Grant was the *Washington Post's* Local Business Editor in the mid-1990s when senior newsroom leaders gathered the staff to announce a new experiment. Reporters and editors were encouraged to try new personal computer stations to access "this amazing thing called the internet," Grant recalled. "They were pretty sure it was going to be a *big thing*," said Grant, now *Post* Managing Editor.

Seems pretty funny nearly 25 years later. But the early days of the internet had plenty of skeptics, including legendary investor Warren Buffett, who passed on the chance to buy a stake in the internet start-up called Amazon, which Jeff Bezos founded and took public at $18 a share in 1997. Buffett didn't understand how Bezos could grow and profit beyond his garage book sales.

Buffett admits that was a dumb move, a rarity for the billionaire dubbed the "Oracle of Omaha" for his investment acumen. Amazon is now a $1-trillion e-commerce giant that sells everything from cribs to coffins, and its shares hover at $2,000 per share. Bezos personal wealth is estimated at $133.5 billion, making him the richest person in the world, according to Forbes' list of billionaires. One of his personal investments was buying the *Washington Post* in 2013 for $250 million.

It's important to understand key events of the late 1990s into the 2000s because it was a digital revolution for both communicators and corporations. The promise of many internet start-ups never happened, while others like Amazon flourished beyond anyone's expectations. At the same time, news organizations were struggling to understand how to convert their news, advertising, subscriptions, production and delivery systems to the internet instead of printed newspapers tossed into driveways each morning.

Upstarts cost traditional newsrooms millions in lost advertising and subscription revenue, resulting in years of layoffs of journalists and others. The timing was especially unfortunate given the deluge of corporate news and scandals that cost investors, consumers, employees and taxpayers billions of dollars.

In addition, the continued ripple effects of the Great Recession of 2008 buoyed Donald Trump's ascent from reality TV to the White House in 2016 because "a group of Americans felt economically and culturally disenfranchised," said Dean Baquet, executive editor of the *New York Times*. "We didn't understand the continued fallout from the financial crisis."

Test Driving on the Digital Highway

The *Post* was one of the first newspapers to go digital with publisher Don Graham investing millions in the project. Grant became the *Post's* first web editor in 1999. But many of the newspaper-side editors resisted change.

Raju Narisetti, a veteran *Wall Street Journal* editor, joined the *Post* as managing editor/digital, in 2009. He tried to bring the traditional and digital teams together, as well as aggregating news from other sources.

"The print side thought the web team was not up to *Post*-quality journalism," he said, "while the web team thought the print team was full of nay-sayers and Luddites."

"He had all the right ideas, but it didn't fit with the newsroom," said Emilio Garcia-Ruiz, who was then editor of strategic projects. "Aggregation was met with newsroom-wide resistance. Beat reporters and their editors were unhappy someone else was on their turf and yet they themselves were unwilling to respond to a piece by a competitor that was doing well."

Narisetti left the *Post* for other senior management jobs and is now a professor and director of the Knight-Bagehot Fellowship in Economics and Business Journalism at Columbia University.

Meanwhile, Google and Yahoo jumped on the aggregation trend and successfully diverted eyeballs and advertisers to their sites. Advertising at medium-sized and metropolitan papers took another big blow to ad revenues when an upstart called Craigslist gobbled up their lucrative classified advertising for jobs, rental apartments and autos.

Craig Newmark founded the site in 1995 as a place for his San Francisco neighbors to find out about the city's arts and tech events. It grew into free ad listings and expanded to nine more cities by 1999.

The site grew revenues by adding paid ads for jobs in bigger markets like New York, San Francisco and Seattle. The company is now in 450 markets. One consultant's report estimates the private company's revenues hit $1 billion in 2019.

Andy Barnes, retired CEO of the *St. Petersburg Times*, now called the *Tampa Bay Times*, is candid about publishers and editors underestimating Craigslist. "Classified ads were not coming back," Barnes said. "I heard that, but I didn't really get it."

As the new millenium arrived, fears of the "Y2K" shutdown of all computers turned out to be much ado about nothing. But the 9/11/01 terrorist attacks on the World Financial Center and Pentagon, as well as the diverted plane that crashed in Somerset County, PA, shook markets, which closed briefly to rebuild after damage from the attacks.

In other Wall Street news, a company called Enron attracted a lot of fans and investors as it grew beyond its main business of 37,000 miles of natural gas pipelines. A subsidiary did natural gas and oil exploration and the company expanded into building natural-gas power plants, an increasingly popular fuel vs. coal. After federal deregulation of natural gas pipelines, Enron continued to grow through acquisitions, such as the purchase of Portland General Electric Co. And its debt load grew. This put pressure on CEO Kenneth Lay to come up with other businesses to crank out profits to keep up with debt payments and satisfy Wall Street's push for better results.

Lay surrounded himself with a handful of cronies who masterminded the increasingly complicated maze of Enron's subsidiaries. His top deputy was Jeffrey Skilling, a former partner at McKinsey & Co. consulting. He built Enron Finance Corp. to bet on future prices of commodities. Skilling created a "gas bank" where Enron would buy natural gas and sell it to consumers. He also pushed Lay to lose the stodgy culture and adopt the hyperactive Wall Street world. Big bonuses drove young MBAs to churn profits as the company expanded to trade futures contracts for newsprint, steel and water.

One of the Wall Street hot shots Skilling hired was Andrew Fastow. He was his protégé and he quickly climbed the corporate ranks to become chief financial officer, according to C. William Thomas, Baylor University accounting professor and author of "The Rise and Fall of Enron" in the *Journal of Accountancy*.

Cooking the Books

At the end of each quarter, companies are supposed to value any contracts, such as those Enron has bought or sold, as either an asset or a liability on its balance sheet. The value is then computed as "fair-market value," or an assessment of what it's worth at that moment, with the change in value booked as a loss or a gain in that quarter's income statement.

Trouble is, this calculation relied on future prices, which no one really knows, so companies like Enron could basically *pick their own numbers*. Even the Financial Accounting Standards Board debated the issue and concluded it was up to the companies to decide how to value the contracts.

"For a company such as Enron, under continuous pressure to beat earnings estimates, it is possible that valuation estimates might have considerably overstated earnings," Thomas said.

Enron's stock took off from $37 at the end of 1993 and climbed to a high of $90.75 in 2000, the year when Enron posted revenues of more than $100 billion. *Fortune* magazine named Enron the "most innovative company in America" five years in a row.

Even the SEC fell in love with Enron, inviting Lay to serve on its advisory team on "new economy" valuations. No one questioned how Enron grew so big, so fast. One reason: the luster of great returns made Enron the Cinderella out of a once-boring utility stock.

Employees, analysts and investors "wanted to believe the company was too good to be true," Thomas said. He blames the greed "born in an atmosphere of market euphoria and corporate arrogance." And it was all approved by Enron's platoon of outside auditors at Arthur Andersen working inside Enron's offices.

The source of much of Enron's meteoric growth was completely hidden and mentioned only in passing in cryptic verbiage in the company's SEC filings. Enron used "special purpose entities" or SPEs, as a way to churn money.

Such SPEs are typically set up as another path to raise funds, or capital. Companies create the SPE, then transfer some assets and related debt to the SPE. The parent company owns a stake in the SPE, so it can use that stake to borrow money and none of the debt shows up on the parent company's financial statements. But the parent company can record a gain from sale of those original assets, which can bolster its quarterly results.

But Fastow figured out ways to make the Enron SPEs even more complicated than basic assets and liabilities. He made them into holding tanks for more and more of the company's troubled assets such as overseas energy facilities and its broadband unit. By doing this, the losses from the company's failures never showed up on its financial statements to the SEC or investors. Enron had *thousands* of these SPEs. And some of them paid executives such as Fastow management fees approved by Enron's board of directors. For instance, LJM Cayman LP and LJM2 Co-Investment LP paid Fastow more than $30 million in fees from its creation in 1999 until July 2001.

Bravo, Bethany McLean: Reporter Shows the Enron Emperor Is Naked

Skilling was named CEO to succeed Lay, who remained as chairman, in February 2001. Global energy prices were falling and there were signs of a recession. In March, the Enron facade began to crack, thanks to a curious journalist. *Fortune* magazine reporter Bethany McLean wrote an article headlined: "Is Enron Overpriced?" The Wall Street veteran turned reporter called the company's financial statements "nearly impenetrable." She raised what now seems like an obvious question, except no one else bothered to bring it up. "How exactly does Enron make its money?"

Enron executives refuted the article, accusing McLean of not getting the facts straight and favoring the opinions of investors. Analysts who questioned Enron's 2000 financial statement footnotes on the SPEs were called derogatory names, according to Thomas.

Meanwhile, Skilling resigned for "personal reasons." One insider was warning her bosses about the lack of disclosure of Fastow's ties to the SPEs. Sherron Watkins, an Enron vice president, wrote a blunt memo to Lay to say she feared the company might "implode under a series of accounting scandals."

The fears came true with a flurry of events between October and December. Enron's first-quarter news release disclosed a loss reflecting a $1 billion charge to write off its failing subsidiaries. Enron shut down some of Fastow's SPEs. That same month, Enron said it changed administrators for employees' 401(k) plans, which locked employees' accounts and kept them from selling any Enron shares for 30 days.

Days after Enron's $1 billion charge, the SEC started an investigation into Fastow's ties to the SPEs and he was fired by Enron. In November, Enron disclosed a restatement of its financial statements since 1997 to reflect the SPEs. That turned four years of rosy results into $591 million in losses and $628 million in liabilities on the balance sheet.

Wall Street hammered Enron's stock, sending it to less than $10 a share. Enron attempted to merge with another energy company, but the disclosures tanked that deal. By the end of November, Enron shares traded at 26 cents per share.

The loss to shareholders was a staggering $60 billion. What they would later learn is just how much Lay, Skilling and Fastow profited from the completely fraudulent accounting. Lay and his inner circle had a lot of incentives to push for profits and pump up the share prices. One of the biggest: Corporate boards grant CEOs "stock options" which entitle the owner to buy the company shares at a lower price, meaning they had an immediate gain. Indeed, between 1998 and 2001, Lay got $300 million from his Enron options and stock at a profit of $217 million. That was on top of his $18 million in salary and bonuses. Skilling also played the options game to reap $89 million in profits from his options.

One particularly offensive perk: Lay received an advance of $7.5 million to buy Enron stocks. Then he was given a line of $4 million in credit that could be repaid in Enron stock. What investors didn't know was Lay was using that $4 million credit line to borrow cash *every two weeks.*

Waking the Watchdogs

Congressional hearings were convened shortly after the bankruptcy filing, Sen. Byron Dorgan labeled it a tragedy for workers and investors because the company "cooked the books under the nose of their accountants and investors." Executives such as Lay and Skilling, neither of whom showed up for the hearing, sold nearly $1 billion in stock while employees and other investors "were set up to take the financial beating."

"Was this just bad luck, incompetence, or greed?...Where was the board of directors when this was happening? ...Were they brain dead, or just kept in the dark?" He went on to question the role of accountants, federal regulators and even his colleagues in Congress for derailing any attempts to regulate such trading. *Business Week's* editorial was read into the Congressional record: "All checks and balances designed to prevent this kind of financial meltdown failed."

One by one, senators took their turn at the microphones to tout what they had just learned about Enron. Sen. Ernest Hollings offered a brief financial tutorial on "special purpose entities." In a classic bit of grand-standing with a touch of candor, Hollings said he would introduce a bill to eliminate "that thing" while adding: "I do not know what it is."

But the impact of "that thing" became quite clear when Robert Virgil, an electrical machinist who had worked for 23 years at Portland General Electric in Oregon, addressed the committee.

"We trusted management's glowing reports of strong financial growth," said Virgil, who then likened it to a house of mirrors crashing down. Virgil said Enron also misled everyone about how long employees were actually barred from trading their own shares. Management said it was just 10 days, but his co-workers found they couldn't access their accounts weeks earlier. Meanwhile, top officers had cashed out their shares.

He read off a list of names of co-workers, with a combined 188 years at the company, who lost about $2.9 million in retirement funds because of the ban. "Their nest eggs are gone," he said. Early estimates put employee losses at $1 billion, but based on his tally of just eight workers, "that estimate is probably low."

The Enron fiasco drew a lot of criticism about the lack of oversight by, well, just about everyone who should be paying attention. Congress passed the Sarbanes-Oxley Act or "SOX" after Enron, and the bankruptcies of WorldCom, a long-distance telecom company, and Tyco, an equipment maker.

SOX imposed tougher standards on auditing, earlier and complete disclosure of anything that could influence financial results, insider dealings such as any extra pay or bonuses, conflicts of interest for directors and the CEO's personal signature on financial statements and tax returns. It also toughened the standards on Wall Street analysts to disclose any conflicts of interest.

One immediate impact of SOX was a change in meetings of corporate boards of directors, once considered a cushy, well-paid gig that required very little effort. Now boards have more legal responsibilities to actually pay attention to what's happening at the company, especially the audit committee. SOX required that at least one director have financial expertise. As one chief financial officer noted in the *Harvard Business Review:*

> *"At the very next meeting of our audit committee, it was a different world in terms of members' engagement level," says one executive. "Some would argue that this intensity should have been there all along, but the fact is, it wasn't."*

The Enron debacle also prompted a lot of second-guessing of auditors, boards of directors, Wall Street analysts and business reporters. Catherine Rentz had a unique perspective as an Enron insider who later became a journalist. After graduating with a finance degree from the University of Texas, Rentz worked as an analyst at Enron for three years. "When it went bankrupt in 2001, it was life altering, to say the least."

She decided to go to the Missouri School of Journalism for a master's degree. Her final project was a content analysis of news coverage of Enron's collapse. "I was curious about how so many got it wrong," she said.

The exceptions were McLean at *Fortune* magazine and Jonathon Weil at the *Wall Street Journal*, who both wrote stories about Enron's questionable financial statements prior to the company's bankruptcy filing.

This isn't something that was fixed after Enron blew up and everyone called for reforms. "The problem is the window dressing at so many companies and accounting firms," Rentz said.

The problem that most reporters face is a lack of time, training and the right sources to help them unravel footnotes and jargon in financial statements. Journalists at local newspapers are completely overwhelmed by the volume of topics they must cover.

With business news, "time is the biggest factor," Rentz said. McLean had the luxury of spending weeks on her Enron analysis. "She pried it open."

As Enron was falling off a cliff, news organizations were shrinking from a convergence of events – ranging from the loss of classified ads to the arrival of Google, among others. Waves of cuts hit hardest at newspapers. The journalists who chronicled the booms-to-busts of industrial titans to tech start-ups, started to write the obituary of the printed newspaper. Knight-Ridder, publisher of the *Miami Herald*, and Times Mirror Co, publisher of the *L.A. Times,* were all sold and downsized.

Thousands of journalists lost their jobs. Plenty of other papers couldn't find buyers and just went out of business. Some news organizations still publish a print edition, but many do it just once a week. Many have gone to digital-only news sites. But another tsunami on Wall Street smacked news organizations in 2008. Ironically, it was a costly lesson on how history on Wall Street repeats itself. To really understand it, you have to review what led to the 1929 crash of the stock market.

Brokers recruited more first-time stock buyers, including women, to put their money into stocks instead of savings accounts.

Retailers and auto dealers extended credit to consumers to provide instant gratification of a new refrigerator, washing machine or Buick sedan.

Banks granted more loans so consumers could take part in the wild expansion of the 1920s stock market.

Those already in the markets took out "margin loans" to borrow more money against the value of their stock portfolios. Credit standards were eased to keep the "Roaring '20s" going.

But fundamental economic problems ended that party. Unemployment was climbing, stock market bubbles burst and the United States plummeted into the Great Depression.

This cataclysmic collapse of the U.S. economy became one of the most-widely chronicled financial debacles as thousands of bankers, brokers, regulators, journalists, politicians and consumers tried to figure out what happened.

Trouble is, the measures that FDR and others put in place after the 1929 crash were being dismantled year by year. In 1999, Congress passed new, looser banking regulations that gutted the Glass-Steagall Act of 1933, which banned banks from investing deposits into stocks or other riskier ventures. The new law, called the Gramm-Leach-Bliley Financial Services Modernization Act, was an after-thought following the merger of Citicorp with Traveler's Insurance, which formed Citigroup.

The deal violated Glass-Steagall, but Citicorp got a waiver to the law from the Federal Reserve, in 1998. Bankers had successfully lobbied that they could only be more competitive if they could offer diversified services, such as insurance and stocks. The passage of banking reforms unleashed a wave of other deals to combine giant financial industries firms.

Meanwhile, the Federal Reserve had to deal with the aftermath of the dot-com bust, one of the contributing factors for a recession in 2001. It was exacerbated by the terrorist attacks on 9/11. In a series of rate cuts, the Fed led by Greenspan slashed interest rates dramatically – from 6 percent down to 1 percent in early 2003 – because unemployment remained high even after the recession ended.

In many markets, housing prices were climbing at a rate of 9 to even 17 percent a year before peaking in the summer of 2006. Wall Street financiers came up with a new financial instrument to profit from the mortgage market.

Traditionally, banks lend a home buyer the money via a 15 or 30-year mortgage. Banks then sell off those mortgages to other banks or financial service companies to recoup the money and keep making more loans to consumers.

Banks and others offered dream deals – set your own monthly payment, loan limits of 125 percent of the home's value, among others. "Subprime mortgages" allowed buyers with lower credit scores and incomes to get a mortgage, but they had to pay higher fees and interest rates. This created a problem because it caused people to borrow more money than they could ever hope to repay, according to research done by Susan Wachter, a Wharton School real estate professor and Adam Levitin, professor, Georgetown Law Center. According to Wachter:

> *"We had a trillion dollars more coming into the mortgage market in 2004, 2005 and 2006. That's $3 trillion going into mortgages that did not exist before — non-traditional mortgages, so-called NINJA mortgages (no income, no job, no assets). These were [offered] by new players, and they were funded by private-label mortgage-backed securities — a very small, niche part of the market that expanded to more than 50% of the market at the peak in 2006."*

One of the biggest "new players" in the subprime lending game was Countrywide Mortgage led by CEO Angelo Mozilo. Countrywide relaxed lending standards and generated massive fees from unsuspecting consumers. Then it quickly unloaded the mortgages to investment banks. A federal investigation of the subprime lending market found that Countrywide sold off 87 percent of its $1.5 trillion in mortgages it originated between 2002 and 2005.

Here's how it worked: A pool of mortgages, or auto loans, are bundled into a security called "credit debt obligations" or CDOs. (The CDOs were modeled after the CMOs issued by government agencies in the 1980s.) The CDO is then sliced into levels, or tranches, based on likelihood of the borrower defaulting on the loan.

The riskier the loan, the higher potential payoff for the investor. Credit ratings agencies ignored the risk and gave the securities a rank of investment-grade, so global buyers flocked to them. One of the dangers of having ratings agencies signing off on the risk is the same companies are paid by the banks for other services, so that conflict of interest tended to inflate the ratings. Housing prices started to tank in late 2006. According to the Center for Economic and Policy Research, markets such as Los Angeles fell nearly 28 percent, while Las Vegas and Phoenix fell 31 percent. The hardest hit houses: the bottom third of the real estate market, where buyers relied heavily on subprime mortgages. In Miami, that market fell 36 percent. Home buyers were quickly "under water," meaning the house was worth less than they owed on the mortgages. What's disturbing is how warning signs were ignored, even by those who are trained to read the economic data, interest rates and market trends as part of their daily jobs.

And those who did predict the coming crash were largely ignored. Robert Trigaux, previously the D.C. bureau chief of *American Banker* during the S&L debacle, worked as a columnist and business editor at the *St. Petersburg Times*, during the Gulf Coast's boom times in home prices in the early 2000s.

> *"Everyone in Florida decided to be (house) flippers. They were borrowing money like mad, buying a house and selling it for 20 percent higher within the year. We were pretty aggressive in coming out with (stories) with warnings that this could end badly. We got blow back from regional and state real estate industry people like you wouldn't believe. They had a PR campaign to call us naysaying*

nancys. If anything, we under estimated the catastrophe that followed."

In fact, the trade group for real estate, the National Realtors Association's 2006 analysis of the housing market laid out warning signs. The group reported that 43 percent of first-time homebuyers in 2005 had down payments of zero dollars – with some getting even more than 100 percent of the loan so they could pay for moving or closing costs.

The revered Greenspan seemed oblivious to the growing problem. The *Washington Post* wrote about Greenspan's reaction to an employee showing him data on the growth of subprime mortgages. In a subsequent interview with the *Post*, Greenspan said he was skeptical because the loans had grown "to such gargantuan proportions" in a short period of time. Remarkably, the *Post* reported that Greenspan said he did not recall if he mentioned this growth in subprime lending to his successor, Ben Bernanke. But remember, Greenspan also told Congress not to worry about any more recessions.

The U.S. economy slid into the "Great Recession" in 2008 after the collapse of the housing market. Much of that was fueled by lenders making subprime loans to unqualified consumers – who didn't have a down payment, good credit or even steady income. Countrywide mortgages and others in the early 2000s were repackaged as junk bonds, although they were rated as investment-grade by the ratings agencies.

So, just to review: What lawmakers did in the wake of the 1929 stock market crash and Great Depression was gutted in the 1980s to help savings and loan associations and Wall Street make more money by making riskier loans.

The Glass-Steagall Act, which enforced separation of banks and investment firms, was diluted in 1999 with passage of looser banking laws that allowed banks to dabble in securities and take bigger risks. This led to subprime lending and the Great Recession, which was the worst economic downturn since the Great Depression.

The true price tag of the housing debacle and Great Recession is difficult to measure, given the scope of foreclosures, as well as big and small companies caught in the wake, and families who lost their homes, savings and jobs. We do know some of the costs.

Countrywide and other mortgage lenders had to slash jobs as foreclosures rose and the mortgage market vanished. Investors no longer wanted to invest in the

CDOs. Countrywide's stock tanked and it reported a loss of $1.2 billion that fall. The bank was sold to Bank of America for $4 billion.

Lehman Brothers went bankrupt. Other banks failed or had to be bought out by healthier competitors. Merrill Lynch, a lead underwriter of CDOs, racked up $51.8 billion in losses and was acquired by Bank of America.

The U.S. government used $7 billion in taxpayer funds to bail out that one company. Meanwhile, consumers lost $16 trillion in net worth and 10 million people lost their homes to foreclosure. One estimate predicted that it would take 85 years of court cases to process the foreclosures just in New Jersey.

Wide swaths of the credit markets were frozen, making it harder to get credit cards or student loans. The fraud of mortgage-backed securities sales even hit employee and consumer credit unions. From 2008 to 2010, 74 credit unions failed.

Mozilo is one of the leading villains of the crash, with *Time* magazine naming him as one of the top 25 people who should be blamed for the financial crisis. Remarkably, the U.S. Justice Department never filed charges against Mozilo. The SEC accused Mozilo of misleading investors while he was dumping $139 million of his own Countrywide stock.

Mozilo eventually agreed to pay $67.5 million to settle with the SEC. But Bank of America picked up much of that tab for him. Analysts say that Countrywide cost Bank of America roughly $50 billion in lawyer fees and other expenses, making the acquisition the worst bank deal ever made.

In a stunning display of clueless behavior after the company's collapse, Mozilo told federal investigators that Countrywide was "one of the greatest companies in the history of this country."

Meanwhile, many Americans are still trying to recover from the recession. Their net worth is much lower. They rent homes instead of buying them. They work two jobs instead of one.

In the wake of the housing market collapse, Congress passed the Dodd-Frank Act, which imposed stricter banking laws, such as requiring banks to boost their level of reserves, which is the shock absorber to cushion losses.

Marty Baron, one-time *L.A. Times* business reporter, saw it unfold as he moved on to eventually become the top editor at the *Miami Herald* and *Boston Globe*.

Advertising revenues continued to shrink as retailers folded and real estate firms bought fewer ads. And few publishers really understood how to transform from printed papers to digital platforms.

The dramatic consolidation of news organizations evoked "empathy and understandable nostalgia" as well as "deep concerns about the implications for the amount of coverage and its quality," said Baron, who became *Washington Post* executive editor in 2013.

"Still, in my view, there was insufficient understanding of why the news industry was under such pressure, what it needed to do about it, why fundamental transformation in a digital era was needed, and why change and hard decisions were needed quickly."

Consumers were rapidly shifting to digital sources for headlines, sports and movie listings. Companies that once bought print ads flocked to Google and social media platforms like Facebook, Twitter and Instagram.

Garcia-Ruiz, now one of the *Post's* managing editors, considers the parallel paths of the legacy newspapers, such as the *Post, New York Times* and *L.A. Times*, and what he calls the "disrupters" like Buzzfeed and the Huffington Post.

The established newspapers stuck to the mission of doing quality journalism, while the upstarts focused on attracting large numbers of readers. As the disrupters built audience, they decided to add journalism, such as AOL's decision to add local reporting via the purchase of Patch Media.

Wall Street loved AOL, which had attracted 35 million users to the internet and email with its ubiquitous greeting of "You've got mail!" By December 1999, AOL had a market cap of $222 billion.

To be sure, some of those high-flying stocks crashed in the dot-com bust. AOL paid $165 billion for Time Warner, declaring that nimble digital upstarts would now conquer stodgy media dinosaurs. But the marriage couldn't weather the recession that hit after the dot-com bust. Two years after the deal, AOL Time Warner wrote off $99 billion related to the deal. Its stock tanked and AOL was eventually spun off. Time Warner was bought by AT&T, while Verizon bought AOL.

Even the venerable *Wall Street Journal* became a page-one story on the changing media industry. Rupert Murdoch's News Corp. offered $5.6 billion to buy Dow Jones & Co., the *Journal's* parent company in 2007.

At $60 a share, the bid was a 67 percent premium over the stock's trading price on the day of the offer. The Bancroft family, which controlled Dow Jones since 1902, initially resisted the offer. But "money talks," Steiger said. "There wasn't anybody who was gonna compete with that."

Journalists shuddered about Murdoch owning the *Journal*, deemed the most-trusted publication in America. They had reason to worry – Murdoch publishes British tabloids featuring photos of topless women. (*The Sun* tabloid in London stopped running semi-nude photos in print in 2015. But readers could still find them on its website.)

Some members of the Bancroft family didn't approve of the deal, noting Murdoch's British newspaper's involvement in a phone-hacking scandal.

Others were happy to take his money. "I'm pretty happy being out of the newspaper business altogether," said Bill Cox, III, a family member.

As Cox learned more about the phone-hacking story, he acknowledged that "We did a deal with the devil and it really saddens me [that] the editorial of this quasi-public trust that has been on the vanguard of world journalism for years is not in good hands. That I am really struggling with."

Matt Murray, *Journal* editor in chief since the summer of 2018, believes the hacking scandal brought about an important change. The *Journal's* strict ethics policy was adopted across all of News Corp.'s newsrooms. "Some people think News Corp. poisoned us, but we changed the entire company," Murray said.

Since Murdoch took over the *Journal*, opinions of the impact on news coverage are mixed. The paper is routinely criticized for going soft on coverage of Trump. A Pew Research study concluded that the *Journal's* page-one coverage of business dropped by one-third from 2007 to mid-2011. The *Journal* shifted to greater coverage of government, politics and foreign news.

The paper has a lot more stories on the high-end lifestyles of the affluent, such as the listing of the $75-million Beverly Hills mansion with ties to Dean Martin. But that same day's paper had a story on the continued fallout from the 2008 financial crisis for many Americans.

Mike Siconolfi, *Journal* Investigations Editor, says the biggest difference these days is the urgency of the 24/7 news cycle. "In the past, there was less competition," he said. "We had more time to develop stories and get out there and meet sources."

It was a luxurious pace when publishing just five papers a week. The format was rigid with page one divided into six columns. The paper did not use photos – just its unique dot drawings. Any change was made at a glacial pace. Writing a headline that stretched over two columns instead of one "was momentous" and reserved for stock market crashes, Murray said.

"The period from the '60s to the '90s when the profession was strong and stable was an anomaly," Murray said. "We were far more secure in our dominance as the business publication of the U.S. We were lackadaisical about it," he said. "We can't live that way anymore."

His team now includes scores of videographers, artists, audience analysts, not just reporters and editors. "We have the same mission statement. We have to be the paper of what matters in business." Like many veteran newspaper people, Murray still says "paper" out of habit, but wsj.com dominates over print. At its peak, print circulation of the *Journal* was around 2 million. It now has 2.7 million subscribers, with 970,000 still receiving the print edition.

News Corp. had to write down the Dow Jones purchase price by half, or $2.8 billion. Since Murdoch bought the *Journal*, the editorial staff was slashed by 700 people to about 1,300. To be sure, it still hires journalists. Murray increasingly looks for specialists who break news at competing publications. Likewise, it has lost some of its tech reporters to the *Post's* expanded tech team in Silicon Valley. Many took jobs at Bloomberg when Murdoch consolidated the operations of the news wires and newspaper.

One constant remains as the news industry continues to evolve: the endless appetite for authoritative and accurate stories.

"We view the world through the lens of business, markets and economics," Murray said. "Those are the forces that drive the world."

Farmland along the Mississippi River Basin became muddy bogs after a 200 percent increase in spring rains in 2019. Reporter Emily Moon of *Pacific Standard* magazine had no shortage of data to cover the story: The U.S. Department of Agriculture's reports on soybeans and corn, NOAA's National Weather Center's rain gauge and the American Farm Bureau's count of how many millions of acres couldn't be planted with corn.

But to bring the story to life, Moon went to Scott County, Missouri to interview Kate Glastetter, who tends cattle and row crops with her father. "The fields are washing away," said the 25-year-old farmer. "It just looks like a muddy mess…"

Moon understood two key principles of business journalism: You have to put numbers into a greater context of the industry and global economy. And the best way to help your audience understand is to "put a face" on the statistics by finding the people who are most affected by the storms.

Beyond the financial statements you reviewed in Chapter Two, it's important to understand some more scorecards, as well as past and current trends to put everything in the proper context. Just as our review of financial statements started with French fries, let's start with a basic commodity – corn.

Corn is an ingredient in livestock feed, groceries and fuel. Farmers mix chopped corn with other grains to fatten up cattle. The livestock are then sold to meat processors Tyson Foods or Purdue, who package it for grocers or restaurants. Consumers buy it at the market or McDonald's. Corn is also the primary source of ethanol, which is mixed with gasoline to reduce air pollution.

For the U.S. corn farmer, sale of their fall harvests will determine if they can buy a new John Deere tractor or make payments on land mortgages. For dairy farmers, who already get lower paychecks for milk sales, selling corn at a lower price is another blow to the bottom line. The low returns are taking a big toll. At least two Wisconsin farms were being were sold each day in 2019. The reason: raw milk now fetches about the same price as 1999, but farm expenses have increased.

Consider the impact of foreign markets such as China, which buys U.S. grains as well as hogs. The country is the world's leading pork consumer and needs U.S. hogs to replace about half of its own herds which died from swine flu. But U.S. farmers have been hurt with each round of tariff spats. The USDA reports that China imported $9.2 billion in ag products in 2018.

"It's all one big story about how policy affects their lives," said Dean Baquet, executive editor of the *New York Times.* He does not want to limit coverage of tariffs and trade wars to Washington politics. Instead, his correspondents are telling it from factories in Shanghai to farms in South Dakota.

"I feel particularly compelled to do that because we're one of few institutions that's big enough to do it," Baquet said. "It saddens me that local news organizations can't. The Lexington (Ky.) paper can't cover coal the way it did 25 years ago. We have to do that."

Understanding Market Metrics

To understand the food chain in covering the money trail, let's go back to the McDonald's chicken nuggets. Long before it makes a sale, McDonald's needs to buy land for a new restaurant, hire a contractor to build it and employees to deep fry frozen chicken nuggets. To stay in business, Mickey D's needs to spend money for advertising, insurance, utilities, more fries and ketchup.

As discussed in Chapter Two, the company's core financial statements give you a quarterly "snapshot" of the key figures – revenue, net income, cash flow, etc. To get an even deeper picture of how McDonald's performs versus competitors like Wendy's, Burger King and Taco Bell, analysts use certain metrics, often measured in ratios. For instance, restaurants look at costs such as how many days it keeps fries as freezer inventory versus selling them.

Some metrics can be useful regardless of the industry. Here are a few:

P/E ratio: Price of share of stock/earnings per share for the year. For instance, a stock that has a per-share price of $40 and posts earnings per share of $4, has a P/E ratio of 10. The investor is paying $40 to get $10 in earnings. When comparing P/E ratios, it's important to judge a company by its industry peers. Companies with higher P/E ratios need to generate the type of growth to justify their higher valuation.

Operating margin: Calculated by dividing operating profit by sales. This margin shows how much money a company earns per dollar of sales after the company deducts costs of running the business.

Revenue growth: Change in revenue vs. the year-earlier quarter revenue divided by the year-earlier revenue.

Debt-to-Equity ratio: This ratio shows how much debt or leverage compared to shareholders' equity. Liabilities/shareholders' equity=Debt-to-Equity ratio.

Research and development (R&D) to sales: R&D/sales x 100 to get percentage. Expect to see a higher percentage for pharmaceutical companies that are spending big bucks researching for next big drug. The flipside is restaurant chains and retailers, which don't spend much on R&D. In those cases, the companies aren't required to report R&D figures.

Current ratio: This is a company's current assets divided by its current liabilities. This shows a company's short-term liquidity. A higher current ratio says the company has a lot of liquid assets that can be converted to cash.

Industry-Specific Metrics

In addition to those basic metrics, specific industries have their own set of measures tailored to their business. These are handy when comparing a company to its competitors, such as looking at Target versus Walmart stores. These are called "Key Performance Indicators" or KPIs.

Let's look at the retail business's KPIs.

Sales per Square Foot of Space

One of the most important indicators is how much stuff the store is selling in each of its locations. This is tracked by "sales per square foot of space" in the store.

The formula is easy: Divide the sales by the store's total square feet of space. For instance, if a clothing boutique has $100,000 in sales for the year from its 1,000-square foot location, its sales per square foot is $100.

The management may decide to reconfigure the store layout to increase that location's sales. Or if things look really bad, that location could be shuttered. For comparison, various market analysts say retailers such as CVS has $666 in sales per square foot. Apple stores, which sell pricey phones and laptops, post $5,546 for that metric.

To be sure, the growth in e-commerce will have an impact on in-store sales, so other metrics are needed to gauge how Target is doing against rivals Amazon and Walmart.

Pedestrian Foot Traffic

This is the total number of people who walk past a store. Seems silly to count people who walk past, but it's actually a way to gauge if it's a good spot based on the demographics of the neighborhood.

Same Store Sales
This figure is often called "comparable store sales" or "comps." It measures how established stores (open for more than a year) are doing year to year. Stores that have been open for less than a year are considered new stores. Sales from the new sites are often skewed by promotions to attract shoppers to the store or reflect lower results if the grand opening proved to be a flop. That's why analysts prefer the comps as a more accurate measure of store performance.

Average Customer Spending (or transaction value)
This is calculated by dividing total revenue by the number of sales transactions. A higher number means a shopper is buying more stuff or more expensive items.

Inventory Turnover

This shows how often the goods on the shelves are sold and need to be restocked. For instance, a grocery store's inventory turnover of milk is likely to be a lot higher than turnover of paper towels.

This number is calculated by dividing cost of goods sold by average inventory for the period. A higher number means the store is selling its merchandise more quickly. This helps calculate how much inventory it needs in the backroom. Keeping too much of a product with low turnover costs money.

Tips from Analysts' and Government Reports

Investment banks and other firms hire people to crunch the numbers on what companies are expected to sell and earn in upcoming quarters. As noted earlier, these analysts get regular briefings from each company ahead of the actual release of quarterly results. Formulas help them calculate the prediction on quarterly sales, net income and earnings per share.

Many are skeptical of the reports, given that investment banks consult with the same companies on mergers and acquisitions, as well as stock or bond offerings. Meanwhile, analysts at the same firm are issuing their reports on the outlook for the company's future quarters and whether the stock is rated as a buy, sell or hold.

But one thing that analysts' reports offer is a detailed breakdown of the company's business, which is a valuable tip sheet for a reporter or communications manager looking to understand the competition.

Seeking Alpha is a popular website that accepts various contributors' reports on stocks, commodities and other topics. For instance, in June 2019 as farmers dealt with muddy fields, Seeking Alpha published Teucrium Trading LLC's report noting a record global demand for grains in the 2019–20 crop year. Teucrium, a Burlington, Vt.-based commodities trader, noted that heavy rains mean less corn harvested. But farmers could see higher prices for wheat and soybean, which can be corn substitutes in animal feed.

Many other sites offer free access to analysts' reports, such as Yahoo! Finance,

Zacks, Nasdaq.com and Reuters. Online brokerage sites offer access to S&P or Morningstar reports to customers. When in doubt, just search via Google to find "free Wall Street analysts' reports."

Don't overlook free government reports on industry trends, such as the Federal Reserve's "Beige Book" report, which is produced by each of its regional banks eight times a year. This is a terrific overview of current economic conditions reported by the 12 districts of the Federal Reserve. The report is based on conversations with merchants, farmers and bankers, among others, to get anecdotal or qualitative examples to help put a face on economic data in each district.

Economists, CEOs, marketing consultants and journalists should always be watching for changes in purchasing behavior, ranging from orders for new 747 jets to moms buying cheaper store-label cereal instead of national brands. These are the early signs of an economic slowdown.

"Leading" indicators predict what's going to happen.

"Lagging" indicators reflect on what has already happened.

"Coincident" or current indicators reflect what is going on right now.

Some examples of each indicator are:

Leading indicators include orders for "durable goods" such as refrigerators, washers and dryers. If consumers are confident about their jobs, checking account balance and retirement funds, they are more likely to remodel the kitchen. If not, they might just slap on a new coat of paint instead.

Likewise "housing starts" measure the number of new houses being built, which shows contractors and developers are optimistic about future sales of new vs. existing homes.

Lagging indicators include the Consumer Price Index, or CPI, which measures the change in prices for a basket of goods in an urban area from month to month. The measure is done by the U.S. Bureau of Labor Statistics and includes groceries, restaurant meals, utilities, clothing and housing, among other items.

Another lagging indicator is the unemployment rate because it measures last month's jobless figures.

Coincident indicators include personal income and "gross domestic product" or GDP, which measures all goods and services produced in the country.

Surveys of consumer confidence are widely-tracked by economists because they reflect Americans' responses to basic questions such as: Do you think your household income will be higher, lower or flat a year from now? Two of the top surveys are done by the Conference Board and the University of Michigan.

Looking at Americans' economic confidence is essential, given that consumer spending accounts for 70 percent of the GDP.

Not all economic indicators are based on government statistics or surveys. But they can be a predictor of how consumers are feeling about their wallets and paychecks. The "Lipstick Indicator" was created by Leonard Lauder, former chairman of the Estee Lauder cosmetic company. Lauder said rising lipstick sales show consumers are watching their pennies. If a woman doesn't want to splurge on a new outfit, she'll buy a new lip color instead.

Another fun, albeit unreliable, indicator is the "Hemline Index" first suggested in 1925 by George Taylor, a Wharton Business School professor. He figured the baring of women's knees with the 1920s short skirts reflected the go-wild, spend-big mood of the "Roaring '20s."

The crash of 1929 and the Great Depression brought a return to a more conservative look of longer, plain skirts. The mini-skirt was a hit in the "conspicuous consumption" era of the 1980s, but disappeared along with much wealth in the market crash of 1987.

But let's not overlook the male version of dubious indicators: Former Federal Reserve Chairman Alan Greenspan believed that increased sales of men's underwear showed a strong economy.

5 | Digging Deeper Into Data and Documents

White House State Dinners have honored visiting kings, queens and other dignitaries ever since President and Mrs. Ulysses S. Grant welcomed King David Kalakaua in December 1874.

But world leaders invited to such fetes during the Trump years often dined among golfers and tourists. The real estate developer-turned-president likes to entertain at his Mar-a-Lago golf club resort in Palm Beach, Florida. That's where he hosted state dinners for the Japanese Prime Minister Shinzo Abe and Chinese President Xi Jinping.

It's not just the beaches and golf course that attract the entourage to the Sunshine State. The jaunts boost hotel bookings, dinner and bar tabs at Trump's hotels and restaurants. The president's routine trips to visit his own properties in Scotland, Ireland and various states prompted even his White House Counsel to caution the president about wasting taxpayer funds on the junkets.

Besides, his trips generate more bookings from a gaggle of business and political leaders who swarm after Air Force One in hopes of meeting the president. Indeed, David Fahrenthold, reporter at the *Washington Post*, tallied up at least $1.6 million in revenues generated from such trips. Yet a few months later, Trump boasted to world leaders that he wanted to host the 2020 G-7 Summit at his Florida resort.

Fahrenthold continues to dig into the story, especially bookings by foreign leaders. His work is a perfect tutorial on following money and exhuming documents to hold powerful people accountable to the public, whether it's a politician, CEO or school board president. Reading about his exhaustive reporting shows the importance of collecting rich details and putting the story into the proper geo-political context.

"Trump is influenced by praise, political support and if you say nice things about him on Fox News," Fahrenthold said. "Money matters to him, too. If Trump is doing X to help the Saudis, I want to see if the Saudis are using his hotels."

And the tales of Trump's business empire turned a bit seedier in July 2019, when Fahrenthold broke a story about a Miami strip club holding a tournament at Trump's Doral, Fla. golf course. Instead of the normal caddies, golfers would pay $450 to $1,800 to have club dancers serve as their "caddy girl" for the day.

The reporter found out about the Shadow Cabaret dancers turned caddies by geo-tagging Trump's properties on Instagram, which popped up an illustration of a golf ball emblazoned with a bright red lipstick kiss.

The club's marketing director said the caddies would be clothed during the golf games. But after dinner, patrons would go to the strip club for a "very tasteful" burlesque show that would feature nude women. Proceeds from the golf event would be donated to a children's charity, the Miami All-Stars.

But apparently, no one informed the charity's management that a fundraiser for children was sponsored by a strip club. Carlos Alamilla, the charity's director, told CNN that he heard about it when the *Post* called him for comment. Alamilla immediately contacted the strip club's manager to remove the charity's name from all ads or anything related to the tournament.

The strip club cancelled the event shortly after the *Post* published the story.

It was yet another blow to the Doral, which lost its top PGA Tour event after Trump entered the race for president. The club's operating net income dropped by 69 percent from 2015 to 2017, according to tax documents the resort filed with Miami-Dade County to support a dispute over taxes.

Fahrenthold also pursued how lower hotel traffic at some Trump hotels prompted them to reduce their room rates. Fahrenthold found that "rates go down and people move in to shoot porn. That's an economic indicator I don't know how to measure," he joked. He found that tip when photos of scantily-clad women posing on beds at the hotels have surfaced on social media.

Fahrenthold is an ace at tracking Trump's money. He won the Pulitzer Prize for National Reporting in 2017 for investigating Trump's claims that he donated millions of his own money to charities. Fahrenthold called more than 420 charities to ask if Trump had, indeed, made donations. His reporting revealed that Trump had given less than $10,000 of his own money since 2008.

One charity that did get a lot of his attention was his own – the Donald J. Trump Foundation. Trump used his foundation's funds, solicited from others, to buy two giant portraits of himself and to settle lawsuits related to his private businesses. The largest gift from his foundation was for remodeling a fountain outside Trump's Plaza Hotel.

"A significant part of any beat is where they get money," Fahrenthold said.

Following the money is part of a journalist's role as an independent arbiter of facts, which is increasingly essential as social media make it very easy to instantaneously spread propaganda, fiction and outright lies. Emilio Garcia-Ruiz, one of the *Washington Post's* managing editors, summed up the importance of journalists as watchdogs of power and money:

> *"As this communications revolution has occurred and humans have changed the way we communicate, it's more important than ever to have truthful, accurate, impartial news. There are so many forces aligned against the truth. It's really important that we maintain our role as an objective observer of society that speaks truth to power."*

Investors and consumers can't count on regulatory agencies to have time or money to be true watchdogs. The SEC, for instance, expects to monitor $97 trillion in securities trading in 2020, a 29 percent increase from 2019. But its budget hasn't kept pace to upgrade technological tools or expand investigations into publicly-traded companies.

> **"**A significant part of any beat is where they get money.**"**
>
> —David Fahrenthold

Journalists' scrutiny of how CEOs or politicians spend investors' or tax payers' funds is even more crucial when budget cuts mean fewer federal, state and local employees enforcing laws. Doing those stories is part of a journalist's DNA.

"As the world gets more complex, we are here for individuals," said Matt Murray, editor of the *Wall Street Journal*. "They need people with the resources to look out for their interests. To hold the powerful to account is one of our jobs. The objective is clear: arm individuals with information to use as they see fit."

Adds Nell Minow, who has worked for decades for tougher corporate governance of investors' money: "We need objective outsiders. Shareholders, boards, business press, trade press, main street press and consumers," should all be "monitoring power and money."

Like many reporters, Fahrenthold didn't set out to do business reporting. But all quickly learn that the money trail is a key route to covering many stories in politics, sports and entertainment, not just traditional business or financial news. And the best reporters' work offers lessons on how to follow the money with the help of documents buried in records at local courts or city halls, as well as the SEC and dozens of federal agencies.

Reporters must pause from texting, tweeting and email and roam around. The only way to put a face on business news is to wear out some shoes – knock on doors of employees who lost jobs in downsizings, retirement funds to accounting scandals and clean water to chemical leaks.

Trash Compactors and Bachelor Bashes

Business reporters, especially at the *Wall Street Journal, New York Times* and Bloomberg News, invest a lot of reporting time and resources into stories about the center of economic power – Wall Street and the big banks. That requires reporters who can exhume documents and tap into industry gossip.

Susanne Craig remembers her job interview at the *Wall Street Journal.* Senior editor Dan Hertzberg gazed out his window to the financial district. "Money, power and greed," he said to Craig. "What more could a reporter want?"

It was a plum assignment for Craig, who was hired by the paper in 2000 to cover online brokerage firms. But she soon realized the best stories meant hours of reading corporate documents filed with the SEC.

Her research soon paid off when she found that employment contracts were especially rich in details on greed and excess. E*Trade CEO Christos Cotsakos was the highest-paid CEO in the brokerage business with a pay and perk package worth about $80 million. That included forgiveness on a $15 million loan, $15 million in company-paid taxes, $29 million in restricted stock and 1.87 million in stock options. But wait! There's more!

The company paid for the CEO's security systems at his house and on his plane, flights to London and the tuition to finish his doctoral degree. No worries for Dr. Cotsakos if the company is sold: He would get a "golden parachute" of about $125 million if a sale results in his dismissal. (Golden parachute is the nickname for exit packages guaranteed to give execs a very comfortable jump from the C-suite.) Retirement looked sweet, too: He would get $8.8 million a year.

Here's the lede on Craig's May 2002 page-one story for the *Journal*:

> *"E*Trade Chairman and Chief Executive Officer Christos Cotsakos yesterday received a Ph.D. in Economics from the University of London. Angry investors say he should go back for a lesson in corporate governance."*

One executive compensation consultant deemed it "a runaway gravy train, and you have to wonder who is at the switch."

Reports on his lucrative pay package hammered E*Trade's stock by 30 percent. The shares traded at $70 but plummeted to around $6 after disappointing quarterly results and the *Journal's* coverage of the CEO's pay.

The SEC documents had some gems about perks for other execs. One had an employment contract that detailed his home needs provided by the company: trash compactor, garage doors and refrigerator. Not to be left out of the fun, the board of directors also voted to give themselves a raise and higher fees just for showing up for meetings.

Her coverage got results: Two days later, E*Trade said the board issued a new contract to the CEO. Cotsakos would not get a base salary for two years and any bonus would be linked to the company's performance. The chief also returned $12.2 million in restricted stock and the $6 million the company put into his retirement account. Still, the CEO remained the highest paid chief in the brokerage industry.

Apparently, there were other issues that irritated the board and investors. The company had spent lavishly for Super Bowl ads featuring the CEO and a chimpanzee. The company sponsored Rolling Stones' concerts. By January 2003, Cotsakos resigned, calling it a mutual decision with the board. His severance was reduced to $4 million.

The story was eye-opening for Craig.

> "It was such an abuse of power and use of corporate funds for crazy,
> personal pursuits. I learned while covering Wall Street that people
> like to live well and spend money on crazy things. It's a way that all of
> them keep score. Who has the nicest house in the Hamptons? All of
> these people have some sort of weakness for something. You need
> to look for that. That is more often than not what is going to trip them
> up."

But the excess of E*Trade was soon eclipsed by a really outrageous story about the lengths Wall Street traders will go to win business from giants like Fidelity.

Three firms – Jefferies Group Inc., SG Cowen & Co. and Lazard Capital Markets – passed the hat to pay for a lavish bachelor party in 2005 at a ritzy South Beach Miami hotel for a former Fidelity trader.

Craig and her colleague John Hechinger wrote the page-one account of the bash, noting that organizers even rented a dwarf for the event. Craig interviewed Danny Black, who runs the website shortdwarf.com and charged $149 an hour to show up at parties to help out staff or mingle with "regular size" people on the party yacht.

Regulators weren't amused about the party for Thomas Bruderman, the ex-Fidelity trader, who was about to marry Sandra Kozlowski, daughter of L. Dennis Kozlowski, the former CEO of Tyco International. (At the time, Dennis Kozlowski was facing felony charges for looting $100 million from Tyco to fund his lavish tastes for a $2 million Roman-orgy party and a $6,000 shower curtain. He was convicted and spent six and a half years in prison.)

The National Association of Securities Dealers or NASD (which is now called the Financial Regulatory Authority, or FINRA) and the SEC opened an investigation into improper gratuities aimed at getting Fidelity's business. NASD rules ban brokers from giving or receiving gifts worth more than $100. And the U.S. Attorney in Boston convened a grand jury to investigate whether brokerage money paid for prostitutes and drugs.

The party bill apparently exceeded the legal limit: airfare alone was $75,000. Fidelity had already dealt with similar problems. Bruderman left the company after ethics violations.

A month later, Craig and Hechinger did another story detailing the $1.5 million annual expense account Jeffries Group Inc. used to treat Fidelity employees to trips to the Bellagio in Las Vegas, free golf clubs and lots of expensive wine. A golf tournament in Vegas cost $120,000 plus a hotel bill for $47,000.

Six months after their first story was published, regulators proposed tighter rules on entertainment. Instead of setting dollar limits, the new plan put the onus on companies to set internal standards which will be reviewed by regulators.

The party spending was "probably more outrageous than we found out," Craig said. "Access to money can be a corrosive force."

Finding some rich details, such as rental dwarfs for bachelor parties, requires some luck, but it's more likely to happen when reporters invest lots of time talking to people and digging into documents.

Being well versed in all the SEC filings is the best way to get a lot of details on a company and its executives. It's best to do this when you're not on deadline so you're ready to pounce on breaking news. The right sources will likely remember that you invested the time and take your call when you're trying to pin down a story.

Sometimes, you can find sources inside the regulatory agencies because their job is to enforce the rules, so they should share your interest in getting the facts on wrongdoings. Besides, they have no vested interest in the company. Likewise, the company's "outside" directors on the board, ones who are not in company senior management roles, are your best hope because they are independent.

The best ones actually understand the financial statements and read company documents. Too often, boards include management cronies, former governors and politicians, who collect their directors' fees and pay little attention to actual business.

"Only in the last 20 years have you seen the rise of truly independent directors," said Charles M. Elson, director of the John L. Weinberg Center for Corporate Governance at the University of Delaware. Beyond being an outsider, Elson stresses the need for directors to also own stock in the company.

"Equity ownership is the linkage between you and the company. And you've got to ask the right questions and have courage. That's what you're engaged to do."

He knows better than most because he made headlines for standing up for shareholders at Sunbeam Corp. Elson joined that board after meeting Sunbeam CEO Albert J. Dunlap, who had read the professor-attorney's articles on director compensation.

In 1996, Elson pushed management to pay all Sunbeam directors in shares and to make them invest their own money in the stock. That way, they have a vested interest in the operation and success of the company, versus just getting cash for their service.

Dunlap was nicknamed "Chainsaw Al" because he fired so many people after buying companies. As Scott Paper CEO, Dunlap fired 11,000 people, or 35 percent of the workforce. Meanwhile, he got $100 million in salary and other compensation when the company was sold to Kimberly-Clark.

He wrote a book called "Mean Business." He borrowed President Harry Truman's line about friends in Washington and tweaked it for Wall Street: "You're not in business to be liked. If you want a friend, get a dog."

Dunlap could've used a dog. Elson and his fellow board members voted to fire the CEO after discovering questionable accounting practices. Sunbeam pumped up sales results by booking sales of grills prior to them actually being sold. In fact, they hadn't even been shipped to retailers.

Shareholders sued Dunlap and Sunbeam, which filed for bankruptcy in 2001. The SEC fined Dunlap and barred him from ever serving as an officer or director of a company. *Time* magazine in 2010, in honor of National Boss Day, named Dunlap as one of the "Top 10 Worst Bosses."

"When he ousted Chainsaw Al, (Elson) became my hero," Minow said. "If every director was like Charles, I could go into another line of work."

Minow helped start several investment firms, including Lens Inc. and Corporate Library, that were outspoken about inept moves by CEOs and detached boards of directors. She successfully brought about changes at Eastman Kodak, American Express and Sears. And Minow successfully lobbied for better disclosure laws so shareholders, customers, employees and regulators know what's really going on inside board rooms.

For instance, the practice of adding celebrities or retired politicians to boards ranks among her top pet peeves. "O.J. Simpson was on five boards," she said. CEOs would even put relatives on their boards to stack any votes in their favor.

Excessive corporate compensation packages is another concern. In 1993, she was researching Borden Inc., then maker of Elmer's Glue and Cracker Jacks. Initially, she was pleased to see that CEO Anthony S. D'Amato wasn't getting a bonus given the company's poor performance. Borden's stock had lost half its value in two years.

But she soon learned from an investment firm manager that more recent SEC filings revealed his employment contract and some outrageous perks. The company paid for two houses and property taxes. Another clause provided the CEO with 100,000 stock options with a price that would be decided at a later date.

The options were meant to make up for the decreased value of his current holdings. By pricing of the options at a later date, the CEO would make greater profits when he exercised them to buy shares. In the interim, the company announced it was cutting the dividend, which made the stock drop even more.

As if that wasn't greedy enough, the contract said if shareholders voted against D'Amato's options, the board would still be on the hook to pay him the equivalent value "It was insane," said Minow, who sent the employment contract to a *New York Times* reporter.

D'Amato was canned by the board in December 1993.

Minow applauds some of the reforms, which largely follow major scandals or market meltdowns. "Enron and the financial crisis were big wake-up calls," Minow said, noting passage of Dodd Frank and Sarbanes Oxley as two positive changes.

Breaking news about the inside-the-boardroom drama takes work. "Board conversations are pretty tight," Elson said. "You've to get to know someone who is willing to talk." Lawyers are often mum, but investment bankers "are notorious for talking."

So are recent retirees, who stay in touch with their pals still on the job. Many companies have employee newsletters that list who is retiring. It can be a gold mine of sources because one talkative retiree can lead to dozens of others. Besides, many kept a copy of the company's internal phone numbers. Another place to find sources is to track down corporations' alumni societies.

The Fahrenthold Method

Using social media proved key in the *Washington Post's* investigation into then presidential candidate Trump's actual donations to charities. Reporters traditionally have guarded their work-in-progress as to not tip off the competition on a big scoop. But David Fahrenthold took the opposite approach when he reported on then candidate Trump's claims about making contributions to veterans' groups and other charities.

Fahrenthold kept a legal pad list of more than 420 charities contacted by the *Post* starting in the spring of 2016 until his story was published in October. Once he exhausted traditional reporting methods of calling, emails and knocking on doors, Fahrenthold decided to turn to Twitter for help from outsiders.

Each afternoon, he would take a photo of his legal pad lists of charities, with updates on what he knew about Trump's last personal donation to the cause. In different colors of ink he would note "NEVER" or "No comment" after the charity's name.

It was a tedious process. "I've now called 313 charities in my search for proof @realDonaldTrump gives his own money away. Not much luck lately" he tweeted at 5:45 p.m. on September 5, 2016.

He found the list helped remind his followers about the story in the deluge of Trump's daily rants about, well, everything. "If you cover Trump's words, you're always just chasing your tail and letting him set the narrative. It's hard to pin him down," Fahrenthold said. "With this, you're judging him by his actions, not his words."

His years of covering government agencies proved that Freedom of Information Act (FoIA) requests for documents is largely useless for time-sensitive stories. "When covering the federal government and you send in a FoIA, you might as well set it on fire," Fahrenthold said. "The timelines are so long you hope it comes back in two years."

He found the opposite happened when he did a FoIA request of local and state agencies and government. While investigating Trump's charitable gifts, Fahrenthold learned that Bedminster Township in northern New Jersey requires a lot of paperwork and approvals even for routine events.

"The police chief and town council have to sign off on a raffle for a quilt,"

Fahrenthold said. In Los Angeles, Fahrenthold learned that the city of Los Angeles levies a 10 percent tax on golf courses, which requires owners to file monthly statements. In Palm Beach, Florida, "they regulate the hell out of everything," he said. "A charitable gala is a 10-page form."

Sometimes Records Just Show Up

After a decade at the *Journal* and another four years covering Wall Street for the *Times*, Susanne Craig wanted to make a break from the beat. "I recognized that I needed to step out of that world," she said. "It felt like it wasn't normal."

She volunteered to become the *Times'* Albany bureau. When Trump entered the race for president, *Times* Executive Editor Dean Baquet asked her to dig into Trump's business interests in New York. "Trump had deep roots," Craig said, "but little influence."

Just as she did when covering Wall Street firms, Craig quickly identified another yardstick the rich use to compare wealth – fleets of airplanes and helicopters. Trump's business acquaintances scoffed at his really old planes. "I was told they were all pieces of crap," she said.

The Federal Aviation Administration should be a reporter's first stop when researching an airplane because each plane is registered with a tail number. That quick check revealed that the registration on Trump's Cessna had expired. "It was only a $5 fee. It got grounded by the FAA because it was not registered."

She commends the FAA as one of the most responsive of federal agencies in turning over public records to journalists because airplanes affect public safety. "Yet so few people are covering this stuff," Craig said. They will check with the FAA when covering plane crashes, but overlook it as a source of documents when covering Wall Street stories. For instance, Craig was able to get jet records from the FAA and piece together where Lehman Brothers executives were holding important meetings before its collapse during the financial crisis in 2008.

As she dug around to tally up Trump's business holdings, Craig persuaded her editors to hire a property search firm to help speed up her search for tens of thousands of pages of public records.

In September 2016, Craig found an envelope containing three pages of Trump's 1995 tax return in her mailbox at the *Times.*

"That's what started this crazy odyssey" of three plus years of digging for more records and sources on Trump's enterprises.

Craig worked with Russ Buettner and David Barstow on a number of stories. Their reporting uncovered 10 years of tax returns filed by Fred Trump, along with bank and other financial records from his deceased father who built the family's New York real estate company.

> *"It started with a simple question. What are the origins of his wealth?" Craig said. "It is daunting in many ways. The hardest reporting target is the guy in the White House. But here is this person whose biography is lie after lie. It was great to find out so much new information. Every day you wake up and feel great because everywhere you go, you find out more new stuff."*

In mid-October 2018, the reporting trio's research culminated in an epic investigative report – at more than 13,000 words, it was one of the longest investigative reports ever published by the *Times.*

The team laid out in great detail a story of Trump's legacy of lies built on the notion that he was a self-made man. In reality, the younger Trump got at least $413 million from his father's real estate empire. The *Times* found that much of the money came from dubious tax schemes and outright fraud.

One allowed Trump's parents to transfer over $1 billion to their children yet avoiding the 55 percent tax rate on gifts and inheritances. Instead of owing the IRS $550 million on such taxes, they paid just $52.2 million.

This transfer of wealth started early for the future president: At age 3, Donald was earning $200,000 a year and was a millionaire by age 8. Despite his repeated claims that he had a small loan from his father to get started in business, he actually got about $60.7 million and didn't repay much of it.

The investigation was awarded the 2019 Pulitzer Prize for Explanatory Reporting. Craig and Buettner continued their investigation of Trump's business empire with a May 2019 scoop that revealed his businesses lost more than $1 billion between 1985 and 1995.

The story was the first time that readers got a more complete look at the president's actual financial history because he has bucked political tradition and refused to release his returns, a common practice by presidential candidates.

Reporters don't reveal sources, but it was clear from the story that Craig and Buettner hit the document jackpot: Official IRS tax transcripts of the 1040 forms obtained from "someone who had legal access to it."

The reporters still took one more step to verify the documents. Craig realized she could match the tax returns to a National Archives database of anonymized income tax returns from 1985 through 1991.

"We had full confidence the returns were the real deal," Craig said.

Holding Powerful Companies Accountable

Asking a lot of questions can lead to a big scoop.

Walt Bogdanich, *New York Times* assistant editor of investigations, recalls a lunch meeting with Bayer executives and various *Times* staffers. PR managers who work for companies based elsewhere occasionally ask for such meetings when the CEO is visiting New York City. "It wasn't clear what their agenda was," Bogdanich said. "There was awkward silence like a bad date."

"What's the big issue in Washington?" asked Glenn Kramon, then *Times* business editor.

One of the Bayer execs mumbled something about railroads.

Bogdanich was puzzled: This is a drug company. Why would they care about railroads?

After the meeting, he called one of the Bayer visitors to ask that question. He learned that Bayer ships a lot of chemicals and rail companies were hiking shipping prices, but no regulators in D.C. were paying attention.

"I thought Teddy Roosevelt dealt with those guys," Bogdanich said, referring to the 1906 passage of tougher federal laws to stop railroads from giving some shippers discounts via rebates.

Curious, he started researching railroads and came across a newspaper story about an elderly California man who was killed by a train as he crossed the tracks. Local police concluded it was a malfunction in the crossing gates that warn people to wait until the train passes.

Bogdanich called the Federal Railroad Administration and asked for more information on the California death. After officials checked their computer listings of such accidents, they told the reporter they had no record of it happening. He learned that the agency relied on railroads self-reporting such incidents.

After some digging, he learned that another agency, the National Response Center, run by the Coast Guard is in charge of tracking data on maritime and railroad accidents based on police reports. "This was a database nobody knew anything about," Bogdanich said. The employees at the center said no reporter had ever called before.

He was able to compare that database to the Railroad Administration records and found "a lot had not been reported" by the railroad companies.

Bogdanich zeroed in on some fatal accidents and talked to attorneys who represented the victims' families. Many of the accidents happen in small towns. "Big media don't cover railroad accidents," Bogdanich said. The stories of deaths "never get out of there and spread across the country." It requires piecing them together to get "a fuller picture of a system that allows this to happen over and over again."

Bogdanich began the series with the story of Blas Lopez, who was delivering a truckload of potatoes to a market in south-central Washington State. He drove across a railroad crossing into the path of a Union Pacific train, which shredded his body and truck.

Union Pacific blamed Lopez for failing to stop.

But the warning signal failed because faulty components should've been replaced more than a decade earlier. A witness confirmed the signal hadn't worked. A lawyer for the Lopez family asked for Union Pacific to inspect the signal. But a rail manager secretly replaced the parts before the inspection. The family's lawyer caught the swap weeks later because he noticed the serial numbers on the parts didn't match the railroad's records.

Bogdanich's seven-month investigation revealed a pattern of such cover-ups where the rail companies destroyed or lost evidence. Union Pacific, the nation's largest railroad, denied that it destroyed evidence. But the reporter found Union Pacific was sanctioned by seven federal and state courts for destroying or failing to preserve evidence in crossing accidents. An eighth judge ordered a retrial. And that was just in one 18-month period.

In one year alone, he found 71 fatal accidents that railroads failed to promptly report, which hurt investigations. Remarkably, he found that twice as many people were killed at rail crossings as have died in commercial plane crashes in a four-year period. And the feds investigated just four of about 3,000 accidents in 2003.

"Railroad companies were playing a significant role in covering up the facts of fatal accidents at railroad crossings," he said. "It was not a pleasant story to tell."

He spent hours with the families of those killed because of the faulty warning signs. After the Lopez attorney confronted Union Pacific with evidence that it had secretly swapped out the defective parts in the crossing signal, the judge called it "egregious" and ruled the railroad could not dispute "this defect caused the crossing signals to fail."

Union Pacific settled the lawsuit, but court documents showed just how arrogant the company acted towards victims' families. Union Pacific, in response to the original lawsuit, said the victim's family should pay the railroad for "loss of use of its locomotives, rail cars and equipment."

Bogdanich's series of stories resulted in changes in federal railroad regulations. He was awarded the 2005 Pulitzer Prize for Explanatory Reporting. He shared his third Pulitzer in 2008 with Times' colleague Jake Hooker for their investigation into toxic ingredients from China that were used to make fake drugs that led to injuries and deaths around the world.

Dave Curley knows how to pitch garbage to a reporter.

Curley contacted Catherine Rentz after reading her *Baltimore Sun* story about volunteer trash collectors saving the lives of two unconscious men with naloxone, an antidote to opioid overdoses. He offered her a tip on more trash-collecting news: A woman organizing neighbors to clean up their South Baltimore housing project.

"It was a story about a real person, not bumbling bureaucrats" Rentz said. Curley introduced her to Jacquelyn Williams, who organized neighbors to recycle glass and plastic jugs. "It keeps the trash and rodents down, and it's better for the environment," Williams said.

Reporters usually complain about PR people, known as "flacks." One reason is a deluge of press releases, emails and calls. "I almost never see" such helpful PR people, said Rentz, who gets at least 10 press releases and story pitches a day. "Half of them have nothing to do with Baltimore."

For Curley, getting a story on the *Sun's* website is gold for his client, Wheelabrator Technologies, operator of a Baltimore plant that converts 2,250 tons of trash daily into electricity for more than 40,000 homes. The company gave out 400 bins and pays "Green Ambassadors" to pick up trash and promote recycling to neighbors.

"Catherine is a good storyteller," said Curley, senior vice president of Sandy Hillman Communications, in Baltimore. "To see it through the eyes of a resident who is benefitting from the program resonates with readers and demonstrates value in the work you put forward to bring it together."

It's important to understand how PR people do their jobs, and how that work differs from journalists. Curley and Rentz show that it's possible to collaborate, but it's increasingly difficult. For starters, PR people can't pitch as many stories to newsrooms because there are fewer journalists to cover more news in a 24/7 digital world. Both communications fields are dealing with public mistrust, heightened by the Trump administration's strategy of misleading journalists, the public and ignoring his own White House advisers.

The president spews vitriol and baits supporters to bully and even punch journalists, who he labels the "true enemy of the American people." The ever-changing cast of the White House press office follows a script parroting his distortions. Those who challenge Trump's behavior or decisions are shown to the door.

"I think people see the White House press secretary is about obfuscation and spin," said David Fahrenthold, a *Washington Post* Pulitzer Prize winner who covers Trump's hotels and golf courses. "Trump elevated it to outright lying. That's not good. They even stopped having press conferences."

The unprecedented behavior by the White House prompted the Public Relations Society of America (PRSA) the nation's leading PR trade group, to discuss the long-term impact on their profession. Indeed, PRSA's 2019 conference attendees talked about an ethics review board to sanction unethical behavior by their peers. Such a board is a mere Band-Aid, given the worst offenders aren't likely members. But leaders of the organization are blunt in their assessment of the "insanity in D.C. and New York."

"We live in a time in our democracy when truth and facts are not all lauded," said Chris Turnbull, director of corporate communications of Carilion, a Roanoke healthcare company and one of Virginia's largest employers. "We are flush with unethical communications where they flat out lie to the public, peers and leaders. It's not even a question of if it's a lie."

To be sure, anyone on the receiving end of a journalist's questions has a gripe about those "hacks," just as often as reporters talk about obfuscation by flacks. It's a natural tension because reporters represent the public in seeking all sides of a story to ferret out the truth. To do that, they ask tough questions of executives and politicians. That's part of a democracy's system of checks and balances – to keep powerful people accountable to shareholders and voters.

PR people, on the other side, are paid to promote companies, causes or politicians through press releases, staged events or social media campaigns. They seek what's known as "third-party" endorsement from news coverage for the client. This is considered "earned messaging." Advertising, on the other hand, is paid placement of a message on TV, print, radio or digital platforms. One expression sums it up: "Advertising is what you pay for, publicity is what you pray for."

Today's communications managers want the legitimacy of helping tell good stories about corporations or people. Most shudder at historical accounts of PR's early days, when even the legendary Edward Bernays crossed the line from selling bacon to hyping propaganda for the Nazis or United Fruits, which later changed its name to Chiquita. Bernays spread propaganda claiming Guatemala's democratically-elected president was actually a communist. Eventually, the CIA armed rebels to overthrow the president, which fueled a 40-year civil war. And it was all for tighter control of a key banana market.

For some, the term "PR" is often perceived as "spinning" a message. For instance, the "spinmeister" or "spin doctor" shapes the public's interpretation of a politician's message. "It was the 1980s when people started to use PR or spin in a derogatory sense," Turnbull says.

Researchers pinpoint its beginning to the coverage of the presidential debate between Ronald Reagan and Walter Mondale in 1984. A *New York Times* columnist described the scene of the press room after the event:

> *"A dozen men in good suits and women in silk dresses will circulate smoothly among the reporters, spouting confident opinions. They won't be just press agents trying to impart a favorable spin to a routine release. They'll be the Spin Doctors, senior advisers to the candidates."*

Many universities teaching PR courses have rebranded them as "strategic communication" classes. Some include the basics taught to journalism students, such as ethics, law, reporting and writing. Others incorporate cognitive behavior studies, multi-media production skills and marketing.

Many who now work in strategic communication roles started their careers as journalists. One reason: they could make more money if they took jobs with major corporations.

"I do think the best (PR people) are, in fact, former journalists," said Tracy Grant, managing editor of the *Washington Post.* "They understand that you're going to ask some difficult questions…and appreciate having a chance to tell their story."

Curley, who worked as a journalist prior to joining the suburban Baltimore agency, has seen his clients' needs grow beyond basic press releases. For instance, if a company is considering a new location for an office or warehouse, his firm is asked to prepare a market report to brief the client on topics such as local politics or environmental concerns. In other cases, a client might want the firm to audit its internal communications operations to see if it needs a facelift.

Another factor that reshaped agency work was the Great Recession of 2008, when most companies had to curb spending on anything deemed non-essential. "First thing companies did was cut back on marketing and that trickled down to PR people," Curley said.

Likewise, the recession meant news organizations lost major retail, real estate and financial services advertising, resulting in newsroom layoffs.

Presidential candidate Trump's obsession with Twitter during the 2016 campaign – and during his presidency – also changed the communications landscape. Instead of issuing news releases to media outlets, he went straight to his supporters via Twitter.

That changed the traditional role of editors being the gatekeepers of the day's news agenda. Traditionally, editors decide what stories get covered and published based on factors such as importance, interest and impact for readers. That decision-making process now includes chasing news tips or checking the accuracy of Trump's tweets.

Every major news organization beefed up its team of reporters and researchers to do such fact checking. As of April 2019, the *Washington Post's* Fact Checker team reported Trump had made more than 12,000 false or misleading claims since taking office.

Managing Ego-Maniacs

While the direct-to-constituent tweets, emails and texts can work for some political and consumer messages, most veteran communication experts advise their clients to use them with caution. For starters, they should avoid the temptation to fire off a reactionary tweets or emails. The last few years have offered plenty of examples of bad calls, including one tweet by a senior corporate communicator.

Justine Sacco, senior director of corporate communications at IAC, was on a holiday flight to South Africa and tweeted about her travels during airport layovers. Just before boarding an 11-hour flight to Cape Town, Sacco tweeted:

> *"Going to Africa.*
> *Hope I don't get AIDS.*
> *Just kidding. I'm white!"*

When she got off the plane, Sacco turned on her phone to find a text from a high school friend: "I'm so sorry to see what's happening." She quickly learned that her tweet set off a fire storm of anger about her racist tweet. IAC denounced the tweet as "outrageous and offensive." Sacco released an apologetic statement. IAC fired her.

Most of the time, however, it's the senior executives who are caught up in their own stupidity. That's when another branch of strategic communication – crisis communications – is put to the test.

Recently, PR and crisis communication agencies have worked overtime to deal with a steady stream of CEOs and other public officials getting caught after years of sexual abuse, harassment and cover-ups to silence their victims. The *New York Times'* investigation into Hollywood exec Harvey Weinstein's sexual harassment of actresses fueled the global #metoo movement as more and more women came forward to share their stories of assaults and intimidation in the workplace.

CBS Les Moonves was ousted as head of the network after journalists broke news about his sexual harassment of women. Journalists Matt Lauer and Charlie Rose lost multi-million gigs after colleagues came forward to tell stories of sexual assault and harassment.

In most of these cases, the damage can spread beyond the predator losing his job and scores of lawsuits against him and the employer. If the public perceives the employer was too lenient about enforcing its own policies to protect women, viewers will change TV channels, drop the company's brands and cash in their stock.

Uber co-founder Travis Kalanick was fired as CEO after a woman engineer wrote a blog post about the climate of harassment and sexism at the ride-hailing company.

Another former software engineer sued Uber in 2019 after she was fired for reporting sexual discrimination and harassment. Uber said her claims are baseless.

Uber's party culture didn't help as the leadership worked towards going public, an IPO that investment bankers expected to raise a record-setting $120 billion.

The IPO raised only $81 billion, reflecting the company's lack of profits, market competition and trade tensions with China, among other core problems. But the former CEO's behavior has lingered as well. The *New York Times* noted: "Though the company has spent millions to improve its brand, Uber's reputation remains tarnished for some users."

Lynn Holley, a former CNN business reporter, University of Illinois journalism instructor and consultant in crisis communications, advises clients to do a "pre-mortem" to anticipate such worst-case scenarios. That way, you have a plan when a crisis actually hits.

One big hurdle that communication staffs face is getting CEOs to trust their media advice as much as they value the CFO's financial briefings or general counsel's legal advice. Just as those senior officers can keep the CEO out of trouble with the SEC, the communication managers can coach the boss on how to avoid self-inflicted negative publicity.

The best advice is basic: Just tell the truth. "If you lie, it will come around and bite you in the butt," Holley said. But speaking the truth to the boss is "difficult to do with an ego maniac" she said.

Many CEOs surround themselves with sycophants who laugh at their jokes. "If you're a CEO, you need somebody who will tell you the truth," Holley said.

Others echo the need for candor, not camouflage. "PR people work too hard at putting a happy face on things," said Chet Wade, principal of AftonRock Communications in Richmond, Va. His advice is candor. Say "we screwed up," said Wade, and make sure it's a sincere admission and not just "for a sound bite."

No Magic Wand Can Sell That Story

Wade worked as a business journalist before shifting to corporate communications. He retired as vice president of corporate communications after 25 years with Dominion Energy, one of the nation's largest energy companies.

For him, anyone considering communications careers must have respect for the role that journalists have in a democracy. He cautions anyone who underestimates the continued influence, impact and reach of legacy news organizations.

When companies need to spread the word about product recalls to protect consumers' safety, for instance, traditional television, radio and newspaper reporters provide considerable reach, especially with those who aren't on social media sites.

"Some people think major media have lost their authority," Wade said. What they actually lost is ad revenues because digital competitors use mainstream media content without having to pay reporters, editors, photographers to produce it. "Look at the original source of the story. It's the major media companies."

And in recent years, the major and most influential U.S. news organizations – the *New York Times*, the *Washington Post,* and the *Wall Street Journal* – have reversed losses and proven that subscribers will pay for accurate, quality information. Even the elusive younger generation that's tethered 24/7 to smart phones turns to those three news sources when big news breaks.

"I have great admiration for reporters and the role they play in society," Turnbull said. "If you don't respect that, you'll never be able to get anywhere" when dealing with the media. His team pitches "good" story ideas each week to various news outlets. Each month, he figures about 60 percent of the news coverage is the company reacting to events, while the other 40 percent comes from ideas his team pitched. He credits his staff's hard work, but also the tone set by the executive suite.

"We have a communicator in chief," Turnbull says of CEO Nancy Howell Agee, whose 47-year Carilion career started as a nurse at the Roanoke hospital where she was born. "She is the one executive I've worked with in my 20-year career that I don't worry about what she's going to say."

When Carilion does face negative news, Turnbull says "reporters won't run the story without a quote from us. We've built a reputation by not hiding stuff. They know they'll get a straight answer."

Reporters have to chase a lot of different news tips and rumors, especially when they're trying to break news about a big corporate merger, or as part of a lengthy investigation. Rachel Abrams covered the Moonves story for the *New York Times* and shared the Pulitzer Prize for coverage of powerful CEOs assaulting women. She values candid conversations with PR people.

"A good PR person does not want to lie to the press and put his or her reputation on the line," Abrams said. If the PR person can't officially comment, she asks: "If I write this, are you going to complain that I'm wrong?"

A trusted PR person responds: "You will not hear from me."

In some cases, the greatest challenge facing the communications team is managing a client or executive's expectations on media coverage. This seems especially prevalent in New York, where corporate clients clamor for favorable ink in the *Times* or *Journal*. Clients in the fashion and high-end luxury retail niches want to be in *Vogue* or *Vanity Fair.*

One New York corporate communications veteran laments such naivete by clients. "They think we can wave our wand and something magical happens," she said. "But if there's no story there, you can't tell that to a giant outlet." Clients need to be realistic: "If you're selling hair accessories, Vogue is not the right place for that."

Curley often explains to clients why the *New York Times* isn't really the right strategic fit, despite the craving for the cachet of being featured in the world's top news site. "Readers of the *Times* are not going to buy your product if you're a regional business in Tucson," Curley said. No one has a secret formula for how to get coverage of positive news, just as they can't hide when bad news erupts. But it's best to have a concise pitch that's based on a story with real people doing something that's different, interesting and likely to have a broader impact on a community.

That's the approach Curley took when pitching the story to the *Baltimore Sun*. His firm could've just issued a press release on Wheelabrator distributing free recycling bins. Instead, Curley knew he needed to pitch a more engaging angle – the woman trying to clean up her neighborhood.

The timing of the pitch was helped by Trump's summer 2019 Twitter attack on Democrat Rep. Elijah Cummings, calling his Baltimore district "disgusting, rat and rodent infested." (Ironically, Trump's son-in-law and adviser Jared Kushner, has ties to the city's deteriorating neighborhoods. His family's real estate company owns lots of apartments that are in disrepair and full of mold and mice.) The *Baltimore Sun's* editorial page blasted back with an editorial headlined: "Better to have a few rats than to be one."

Reaction to Trump's attack prompted volunteers from other states to show up and help clear city streets of debris. Baltimore city leaders were already working on reducing trash in public housing since 2017. In Brooklyn Homes housing complex, the cleanup has cut the number of rat burrows to 38 from 400 when the program started.

"Every city of any size in America struggles because resources are limited," Curley said. "People have to take on challenges" to unite in a common cause and "great progress can be made."

Too Good to Be True

PR people send scores of press releases to editors, gushing about the latest fast food sandwich. Editors react the same way they do when someone calls the *Miami Herald* to say it's sunny in South Beach.

It's not news.

But get this: Even the *New York Times* occasionally will cover a new chicken sandwich. That's what happened in the summer of 2019 when Popeyes' unveiled a deep-fried chicken sandwich. The $3.99 sandwich debuted with good sales.

Customers on social media suggested this new lunch could clobber the beloved Chick-fil-A sandwich. The folks at Chick-fil-A responded with this tweet: Bun + chicken + pickles = all the love for the original.

Popeyes' marketing chief huddled with his colleagues to brainstorm a response to the competition. They settled on simplicity, tweeting: "…y'all good?"

That set off a full-scale food fight on social media with #ChickenSandwichWars.

Customers flocked to Popeyes to buy the sandwich. Employees told *Business Insider* that all hands were in the back assembling sandwiches, neglecting other chores, like washing dishes and cleaning floors.

The chain started to run out of the sandwiches, which annoyed the crowds of hungry customers. The chaos and increased work proved too much for one Newark, N.J. employee. She quit in the middle of her shift.

Less than 10 days after the sandwich was launched, the chain announced that a lack of chicken suppliers forced management to take the sandwich off the menu, at least until it restocks.

But creativity struck again.

Popeyes' started another social media buzz by encouraging patrons to bring their own buns and build a similar sandwich using its chicken tenders. Even the *Washington Post* covered that twist of BYO bun. So, this could explain why those sandwich press releases keep coming in by the dozens.

A Conversation With Dave Curley:
Journalist Turned Strategic Communicator

Every so often, you interview someone and think: Shut up and let him tell the story.

In that spirit, here's an edited excerpt of my conversations with Dave Curley, senior vice president of Sandy Hillman Communications in Baltimore. He was generous with his time and thoughtful in his responses about the state of communications.

Q: What's the agency's role in this digital deluge of free, paid, real and fake information?

A: *It is our responsibility to serve as honest brokers of information. At a time when inaccurate material is widely available and actively promoted on the internet, on select broadcast programs and in some traditional print outlets, we have to carefully consider the veracity of every source we cite and every contact we make.*

When we are skeptical of a particular data point, resource or message, we must not amplify it until it has been properly vetted and established as reliable. Given the vast amount of information currently available – and the pace at which new material arrives – we have to be more discerning than ever.

This is true of anyone who makes their living in the field of communications – from a journalist to a marketer to a public relations officer.

Q: Talk about the importance of having the ear and trust of your client or CEO.

A: *I would suggest CEOs who don't trust their PR people as much as their attorneys should be looking for new PR people.*

That isn't to say CEOs should never take the word of the general counsel over the ranking public relations officer. There are cases, for example, in which the public relations team might initially lobby for the release of specific information in the interest of corporate transparency only to learn from the general counsel that doing so would violate an obscure law.

This is not uncommon in matters of cybersecurity. And disclosure laws can vary materially from state to state – let alone country to country – making such considerations all the more complex for organizations that operate nationally and internationally.

Q: Can you give me some examples of the good, the bad and the just plain ugly in dealing with journalists?

A: *We can have a longer discussion about this, but a few initial thoughts:*

The good: *Most journalists are genuinely concerned with getting the facts right. As a result, most journalists are interested in maintaining strong business relationships with media relations officers who provide reliable, fact-based information in a timely fashion. Most journalists respect media relations people who can help them do their jobs better – find new insights, discover previously unreported information, provide deeper understanding of a particular issue or trend.*

The bad: *Journalists are increasingly being assigned to cover multiple beats, increasing the odds they will have limited knowledge about a specific industry or subject matter. These increased reporting responsibilities also put a greater demand on their time, adding to deadline pressures, increasing the focus on breaking news and limiting their availability to consider feature pieces.*

The ugly: *This diminished focus on specialty, combined with increased deadline pressure, leads to important errors of fact and lack of context. In rare cases, journalists are seemingly incapable of setting aside conscious or unconscious biases, resulting in coverage that doesn't reflect the facts in proper context. The insatiable quest for eyeballs is leading some journalists to write irresponsible headlines, overstate concerns or otherwise attempt to sensationalize their reporting.*

Q: What advice do you have for journalists working with PR professionals?

A: *Think of us as sources, not "flacks."*

Establishing strong business relationships built on mutual trust can lead journalists to more sources and better stories. It can also lead to exclusives.

Good media relations people provide journalists with information, context and insight that results in a deeper understanding of a particular subject. Good public relations people also provide access to senior executives, subject matter experts and other contacts who can further advance a story – or demonstrate there is no story where one was initially thought to exist.

Journalists spend significant time running down leads and rumors. Trusted media relations professionals can end a wild goose chase quickly. They can also confirm a significant lead and point to resources or contacts that can help tell the story. That having been said, wise journalists distinguish between good media relations people and bad media relations people – those who push out irrelevant or unworthy pitches, bombard reporters' email with news releases about items/events of little consequence, etc.

---

7 | Ethics and Common Sense

Ellen Pollock, business editor at the *New York Times*, is tired of PR people trying to stifle reporters doing their jobs.

"It happens a million times," said Pollock, previously Bloomberg Business Week editor and a long-time *Wall Street Journal* editor.

Pollock recalled how one company's PR manager "freaked out" about calls from a *Times* reporter. Pollock got a phone call from the PR person – with an attorney and crisis consultant also on the call – who demanded to review what *anybody* told the reporter.

Pollock reminded the PR team of the *Times'* extensive fact-checking, and that only editors review stories. "It's what we do," she said.

Next came an email asking Pollock to confirm her refusal of the request.

"They were trying to trap me into saying something," Pollock said.

Her response: *"This is a silly email."*

At the *Washington Post*, Tracy Grant, one of the newsroom's managing editors, said any such demands in "crazy, outraged emails from PR people" are referred to her or the newsroom's legal team. "My lawyer is my best friend."

Such requests are stunningly naïve, given the First Amendment's protection of a journalist's role as an independent arbiter of news. As *Times* patriarch Adolph S. Ochs said in 1896: the *New York Times* covers the news, "impartially, without fear or favor."

That means reporters don't rely only on corporate press releases. They interview union organizers, employees, competitors, Wall Street analysts or environmental activists. One source doesn't get the right to silence others who disagree.

On the other side, PR people are paid to protect and enhance the company's image and stock price in service to management or clients. So they want to soften opposing voices in the high-stakes persuasion of investors, consumers and regulators.

In some cases, the sides find common ground, such as getting a reluctant CEO to talk to the reporter. Business journalists always want to hear from decision-makers, not gatekeepers, so a CEO's quotes will be featured prominently in the story. And letting other employees, at all levels, speak for themselves can be a powerful persuader both inside and outside the company. That can be "a symbiotic relationship," said Lynn Holley, who worked as a journalist, university instructor and now as a crisis communications consultant. "But most don't see it that way. It's *us* versus *them*."

Seeking the Truth

To be an effective corporate communicator, it's important to understand how professional journalism is built on ethical behavior in reporting, writing, publishing or broadcasting news. Journalists at credible news organizations seek the truth by gathering information from three main sources: Their own observations of the world around them; interviewing those with first-hand knowledge of events; and reviewing documents from trials, government regulators or a company's own files.

Prior to the 2016 presidential campaign, the term "fake news" was used mainly to describe the supermarket tabloid fodder on Elvis being spotted at a donut shop in Michigan. The phrase actually dates back to the 1890s when rival newspapers would criticize the other of fabricating content. But the Trump campaign extended the phrase to cover anything that didn't fit his narrative of reality or what his handlers called "alternative facts."

Accusing reporters of making up news overlooks a basic reality in professional newsrooms: ***Journalists who make up things get fired***.

Indeed, *Times* reporter Jayson Blair resigned in 2003 after editors and competitors discovered he fabricated and plagiarized dozens of stories. The *Times* published a page-one investigation into Blair's deception, which showed how the reporter had numerous warnings about accuracy. One editor had warned colleagues a year earlier that Blair should no longer write for the *Times*. Soon after the report became public, Executive Editor Howell Raines and Managing Editor Gerald Boyd resigned.

> **"**It can take you a generation to build a reputation and you can lose it in a day.**"**
> —*Paul Steiger*

"Accuracy and fairness are more important than anything else," said Paul Steiger, former managing editor of the *Wall Street Journal* and founder of ProPublica.

"It can take you a generation to build a reputation and you can lose it in a day."

Putting Events in the Proper Context

In addition to getting the facts straight, journalists must put events into the proper context so readers can gauge the impact, relevance and significance. Think about fire fighters' response to calls for help. If it's a grease fire at the local diner, that's likely to be a one-alarm fire, meaning only one crew is dispatched to extinguish the blaze. If a fire has engulfed a 10-story apartment building, it's likely a four-alarm event that requires more help because of the scope and number of tenants.

Journalists must gauge the impact of news events and cover them accordingly. Did a company's stock drop two percent on a day when all of its peers in the tech sector are also down? Or did the stock tank 25 percent after the company disclosed it's under investigation by the SEC?

Another aspect of seeking the truth is to give the readers as much information as possible on the source. That way, readers can decide if it's credible. Too often, sources seek to remain anonymous so they won't take any grief from a boss. What's really ridiculous is when the corporate or political PR person wants to be anonymous, even when they take the podium at a public news conference.

Sources asking to talk "off the record" is another way to dodge responsibility for what they say. At the *Times*, Pollock doesn't hesitate to cut off such conversations. "People go off-the-record way too much," she said. "There are times when I'm telling them: 'No, we're not talking. It's useless.' "

Allowing someone to be anonymous should be reserved for those who would be physically in danger or lose their jobs if identified.

Sources interviewed and quoted for stories must reflect the diversity of people and places who are affected by the news. Too often, reporters quote the same people over and over again. Sometimes, that's because of the pressure of deadlines and juggling multiple assignments and features at the same time.

When time allows, the best stories "put a face" on corporate news by going to the small towns, factories, bars and churches to interview workers hurt by corporate cost cutting. In doing such interviews, journalists must remember that very few have the extensive media training given to CEOs, so it's extremely important, in the interest of fairness, that they take the extra time to explain who they are, where they work and why they're asking questions.

Journalists cannot expect the public to respect their ability to write fair, accurate and balanced stories if they are swayed by those they cover. For instance, journalists cannot accept gifts, favors, free plane tickets or anything that creates a conflict of interest. Beyond those obvious ones, journalists have to police their behavior to avoid even the perception of a conflict. That's why journalists do not put political campaign signs in their yards.

Newsrooms must avoid the influence of those who advertise in the publication, website or broadcast. The largest news organizations, such as the *Journal, Times* and the *Post*, are not swayed by fear of lawsuits or lost advertising. But many smaller news company owners or publishers will self-censor the news coverage because they don't have the deep pockets to cover legal costs or lost ad revenue.

News organizations have increased their efforts to be more transparent about their work with readers and viewers. Editors at the *Times* will publish notes to readers explaining how or why they did a story. This answers a lot of questions and can increase the newsroom's credibility with the public. Likewise, it is essential that newsrooms correct any errors, such as updating the story on the website and noting the specific error in the original version.

Shared Beliefs With One Big Difference

The Public Relations Society of America's code of ethics has many of the same standards as the SPJ's code for journalists. The PRSA wants its members to maintain the highest standards of accuracy and truth, correct errors and avoid conflicts of interests.

The difference in the codes reflects the biggest difference in the two professions: PR people are *advocates for the company or person they represent.* But, the PRSA code also includes standards about not deceiving the public about a client's financial condition or the safety of its products.

Just like journalists, however, PR people don't give polygraph tests to find out who's really telling the truth. Imagine how the PR folks at Enron felt when they learned about the massive accounting fraud would tank their entire company.

As the person who has to face the TV cameras, as well as colleagues, it can be a very tough job, even at well-regarded companies.

"There were two people at the company who were responsible for every big and bad thing," said Chet Wade, Dominion Energy's retired vice president of corporate communications. "The CEO and me. We never got a pass from any stakeholder group."

One topic that both journalists and PR people agree on is the importance of training CEOs and other clients to understand that news organizations pivot to cover different aspects of a company.

For instance, the wildly-successful technology companies, such as Apple, Facebook and Amazon, have enjoyed a long stretch of time when reporters were most interested in covering the latest gadgets like iPhones. Every quarter's results delivered strong profits, and both Apple and Amazon became the first companies with a trillion dollar market capitalization.

Matt Murray, editor of the *Wall Street Journal*, has seen the dramatic shift in how CEOs and PR people react to stories.

"CEOs who want to attack us publicly have a forum" via media critics or emails to competing news organizations, Murray said. One example was Apple CEO Tim Cook's reaction to the *Journal's* coverage of a senior executive leaving the company. "He didn't even talk to me or any of us. He just blasted us" but he never denied the story. "It's a battle of spin and counter spin" that goes nowhere, Murray said.

Silicon Valley enjoyed a long honeymoon with many reporters, who were interested in only testing the latest gadgets. But lapses in the protection of consumers' data have prompted more aggressive coverage of the companies. That change has created a bit of "whiplash in PR shops in Silicon Valley," Grant said.

One veteran corporate communications consultant lamented how some major tech companies' quest for profits means they compromise their ethical standards. Along the way, they lose the trust of employees, customers and investors. Besides, lawsuits follow after the breach is revealed.

He uses the example of Facebook's numerous blunders – such as its failure to protect consumers' data from the political research firm Cambridge Analytica or its previous practice of giving advertisers access to certain people based on race or gender.

Facebook said it has taken steps to safeguard customers' information and stop the targeted advertising. Meanwhile, the company faces a variety of lawsuits and a Congressional inquiry into its business practices.

"From a business perspective," the consultant said, "their operations could be impacted because they didn't operate in a trustworthy fashion."

To read the complete codes of ethics, go to:

https://www.spj.org/ethicscode.asp

https://www.prsa.org/about/ethics/prsa-code-of-ethics

P&G&Me

Procter & Gamble CEO Ed Artzt screamed a lot each time I broke company news in the *Wall Street Journal*. But he really went ballistic in the summer of 1991 when I wrote about a senior executive leaving P&G following crappy sales in its food and beverage business.

Artzt ordered his security folks to search company phone records to see who was leaking information to me. When that failed, P&G turned to the Hamilton County prosecutor to convene a grand jury investigation into the news leaks. Subpoenas were issued to check the phone records of 800,000 homes and offices – about 35 million phone calls – to find any calls to my home or the *Journal's* office.

It was an unprecedented attempt to stifle news coverage. And P&G managed to keep it quiet until I got a call from an acquaintance in Cincinnati.

"I just spent the morning at the police station because of my calls to you," he said.

Paul Steiger, *Journal* managing editor, alerted our attorney Dick Tofel, who contacted P&G's general counsel to protest the company's invasion of privacy and abuse of power. But P&G didn't back down. Steiger told us to have the phones checked for bugs.

The *Journal* editors assigned a colleague to write a story about P&G's tactics, such as the use of law enforcement to silence employees and bully journalists. It was very strange to suddenly be in a story instead of writing it.

That weekend, I went to my hometown for a high school reunion. I knew I'd better warn family members before the story came out, but I dreaded explaining to my elderly mother why the Cincy cops were investigating my phone records.

Her reaction was worse than I imagined:

"Someone's going to kill you," she whispered.

I told her not to worry, explaining that P&G's CEO was just playing hard ball.

That's it!" she yelled, slamming her coffee cup on the kitchen table. "No more Tide in this house!" I told her she'd also need to dump her coffee cup, pointing to P&G's Folgers can on her counter.

The *Journal* ran the story on page one Monday. "This was a big, hairy deal," Steiger recalled. 'Nobody knew what P&G did until we put it on page one. They became the laughing stock. P&G f***ed up and everybody knew it."

P&G officials deemed the phone investigation as crucial to protect its "trade secrets" citing an obscure Ohio law intended to protect proprietary information, such as the formula for Crest toothpaste. But they forgot the obvious facts: The First Amendment protects a journalist's right to cover news, as well as citizens' rights to talk to a reporter.

P&G's "trade secrets" excuse didn't work well.

The *Journal's* editorial page blasted P&G's "sinister" tactics and use of cops to harass people. First Amendment attorneys volunteered to represent the *Journal* and me if we wanted to file a lawsuit against P&G, among others involved. The Society of Professional Journalists wrote to Artzt condemning his "prosecutorial and police fishing expedition" and attempt to censor the media.

Cincinnati Bell customers and local taxpayers questioned P&G's invasion of their privacy, as well as use of tax dollars, county prosecutor and detectives' time for a multi-billion dollar titan's spat with a reporter.

Steiger recalled the next call with P&G's PR guy and the company lawyer.

"They desperately wanted to call a truce and offered to issue a conciliatory statement" about the investigation. Steiger reminded the P&G duo that this story, like all topics, would fade in time, assuming that "another shoe wasn't going to fall off this centipede."

The PR manager quickly assured him that all had been revealed. But the lawyer interrupted to say:

"Well, there is one more thing. The cop who provided the phone records" also worked at P&G.

"We're going to report that," Steiger said with a laugh. Turns out, 30 cops moonlighted as P&G security guards that year.

In early September, William Safire, a former aide to President Nixon, devoted his *New York Times* column to comparing P&G's phone caper to Watergate. He interviewed Artzt for the piece and learned that the CEO was backing down. "We made an error in judgment. We regret it."

Safire quizzed Artzt about the ethics of the phone search, but Artzt still maintained it wasn't improper.

"He still doesn't get it," said Safire, who wrote that P&G's outside directors had an obligation to commission an independent report before the October board meeting and "not turn a morally blind eye to a corporate culture that confuses doing stupidly with doing wrong. Take it from an old Nixon hand: Full disclosure now will save P&G headaches later." Safire said.

Later that month, CEO Artzt and his top PR managers met with me and *Journal* editors at the *Journal's* New York headquarters.

Artzt was subdued, then looked at me and said:

"I thought we were friends."

"My friends don't get the cops to get my phone records, Ed," I replied.

P&G later learned that I had been researching a book about the company's tactics to win at all costs. Apparently, the New York book publishing circuit has its share of leaks, too. Only a few editors had the proposal, but P&G officials got a copy. Once again, the PR guy wanted Steiger to take me off the P&G beat. Steiger gave his usual answer: "Alecia will keep covering P&G until she asks to stop."

The *Journal* gave me a leave of absence so I could dig deeper into P&G.

The company's PR people refused to answer even basic questions, including my personal favorite: PR folks denied that the cafeteria sold Jif and banana sandwiches for 75 cents. I guess the lunch menu must've been another one of those "trade secrets."

But hundreds of current and former employees wanted to share their stories. Those interviews, along with information from hundreds of internal P&G documents, told the story of a corporate bully – and much worse.

The most disturbing part of P&G's story was its sales and marketing of Rely tampons, despite dire warnings about the product's link to deadly toxic shock syndrome. In 1980, at least 42 women died from toxic shock syndrome, many of them after using Rely.

Despite P&G's stone-walling on basic questions. CEO Artzt agreed to meet with me to hear what people had to say about his tenure. He agreed to be interviewed for the book, noting that he wanted to provide balance to stories I'd heard from his employees, who nicknamed him "the Prince of Darkness."

Soap Opera: The Inside Story of Procter & Gamble, was published in 1993. The book was also translated into Chinese, Japanese and German editions. The book even showed up as an $800 question on *Jeopardy!*

P&G never figured out who leaked me any news. And more than two decades later, I still get quite a few phone calls.

8 | Don't Be Stupid: Understanding Securities Laws

The *Wall Street Journal's* "Heard on the Street" column has the power to make a stock soar or sink. It can also tank a reporter's career and land him in jail.

That's what happened to R. Foster Winans, a *Journal* reporter, who routinely leaked the topic of the next morning's Heard column to confidants Peter N. Brant and Kenneth P. Felis at Kidder, Peabody & Co. By disclosing which stock got a good or bad review in the Heard, the brokers could buy or sell based on the news that would send the stock up or down. That's an illegal practice called "front running" or making trades based on insider information.

"People on Wall Street were watching the trades and saw that they tracked what was in the Heard column," said Paul Steiger, who was editor of the *Journal's* markets and economics coverage in the early 1980s when the scandal was brewing. "It got passed along to the watchdogs in the exchanges and the SEC."

"They had him dead to rights."

The scandal started before Steiger became markets editor, but he was called to testify in the resulting criminal trial. Foster "saw other people getting rich" Steiger said. But he adds: "Foster didn't make much money from it." Indeed, the broker paid Winans just $31,000 of the $690,000 in illegal profits.

Brant was fined and was sentenced to eight months in prison, while Felis got a six-month sentence. Winans was sentenced to 18 months but served only nine months. "People are so foolish to think they can get away with it," Steiger said. "If someone is going to steal, they're going to get caught."

Winans wrote a book *Trading Secrets: Seduction and Scandal at The Wall Street Journal.* He was charmed by Brant's wealth and wanted to be his friend. Years later, Winans admitted that selling information from the Heard column was a stupid move. "I used something that didn't belong to me to enrich myself," he wrote in a 2011 column in *Business Insider*. But he considered the prosecution to be akin to "killing a mosquito with a howitzer."

The Winans' scandal happened more than three decades ago, but the impact lingers in the *Journal* and other news organizations' strict guidelines about protecting unpublished information related to stocks. For instance, *Journal* news employees must avoid any hint of profiting from their reporting on companies. Reporters or editors, for instance, who know about information prior to publication must wait an extra three trading days *after* the story is published before making any investment decision that could appear related to the story.

Journal reporters are cautioned about holding any individual stocks, even those unrelated to the companies, industry or beat they cover. Doing so "may prevent them from taking on additional assignments" notes the *Journal* parent company, Dow Jones & Co., in the Code of Conduct. *(https://www.dowjones.com/code-conduct/)*

Even Outsiders Are Insiders

Often times, it's easy to avoid breaking insider trading laws. For instance, corporate officers or directors are privy to upcoming deals, so it's obvious they shouldn't talk or make stock moves based on what they know.

But the law also extends to their friends, business colleagues and relatives, so it's especially important to not let the information slip during cocktails at the golf course. And don't forget all the folks who handle the mountain of paperwork related to deals: bankers, lawyers, outside PR consultants and even those running the copier machine need to be briefed on insider trading laws.

The chances of people profiting from insider information have grown because of the vast network of people connected to the day-to-day work of a company. Plus, email and texting make it very easy to quickly share information around the globe.

The law covers even routine information, not just mega deals. Anything that's deemed "material" information, such as quarterly earnings, stock splits and buybacks qualifies as insider information until disclosed publicly.

In addition, the SEC cracked down on "selective" disclosures of material information by company CFOs or investor relations managers to a privileged few before the general public. For instance, it was a common practice for some Wall Street analysts or large institutional investors to get phone calls prior to the company's press release or 8-K filing.

In 2000, the SEC made this illegal with the passage of "Reg FD" or fair disclosure. To avoid breaking the law, companies must disclose anything material via press releases, the 8-K filing, a statement on the company's website or on social media. The information can be shared on a conference call, if the media are notified in advance.

The use of social media platforms is a relatively recent addition to acceptable disclosure methods. And it has been a source of great aggravation for the SEC, especially when CEOs such as Elon Musk at Tesla go rogue.

In early August 2018, Musk tweeted a message to combat the short-sellers who predicted that Tesla's next quarter sales of electric cars would fall short of targets.

> *"Am considering taking Tesla private at $420. Funding secured."*

The tweets sent Tesla's stock up 11 percent to $379.57 a share.

Reporters immediately texted: *Are you serious?*

Another said: *"It seems like you are dancing into some pretty tricky legal territory by messing about with the markets this way."*

The SEC soon accused Musk of publishing false and misleading statements via his tweets. The case was settled a few days later with Musk and Tesla paying a $40 million fine. He also agreed to get his board's OK before he posted any material information on social media.

It didn't take long before Musk became combative about the SEC. He was interviewed on "60 Minutes" and said he wasn't getting pre-approval for any tweets.

> *"I do not respect the SEC, "* he said.

Once again, he tweeted in February about car production numbers before they were made public. The SEC sought a contempt of court order against Musk. By spring, the SEC and Musk agreed to tighter standards on his postings.

A CEO fighting with the SEC shows the board of directors is failing to do its job as the ultimate management watchdog. One big problem at Tesla is several of the directors have financial or family ties to Musk. His brother, Kimbal Musk, is a director. Antonio Gracias, investor in Musk's other companies, Solar City and SpaceX, is also a director.

The SEC required Tesla to add two outsiders to the board, along with replacing Musk as chairman. But few believe those moves change Musk's tight grip over the company. Besides, dozens of executives, including five senior financial officers, resigned in 2018 and 2019. His VP of corporate communications and investor relations director both quit. So did several of his top lawyers.

"Musk's captured board is one of the biggest threats to Tesla and its legitimacy and corporate governance," said one securities attorney. "He gets to still be the king when he has a bunch of sycophants surrounding him."

Former SEC chief Mary Jo White, speaking to a Stanford University gathering on corporate governance, reminded corporate directors in the audience of their gate-keeping roles. Senior management, along with the board of directors, set the "tone at the top" that guides all others at the company.

Silicon Valley has lots of innovative leaders who do well at the invention stage of creating a product, but then struggle once they become CEO of a publicly-held company. That's where the directors need to make sure the company founder is actually right for the top corporate job. "Deficit corporate cultures are often the cause of the most egregious securities law violations," White said.

Indeed, SEC officials say that a common denominator in many of corporate America's biggest frauds has been the failure of gatekeepers – directors, outside auditors and outside attorneys – to identify and stop wrongdoings.

Perhaps the only good thing that happened after major corporate debacles such as Enron, WorldCom and the collapse of the U.S. housing market was enactment of stricter laws on corporate accountability. The Dodd-Frank Wall Street Reform and Consumer Protection Act became law in 2010 in hopes of preventing future financial debacles like the 2008 financial crisis.

As part of the reform, the SEC created a whistleblower program so insiders can tip off investigators to fraudulent behavior. The agency got more than 3,000 tips a year, including some that led to criminal actions. In such cases, the tipster can get up to 30 percent of the fines paid. In one case, the SEC awarded a whistleblower $50 million.

The law also provides stiffer penalties if corporations try to bully, demote or fire those who report wrongdoings. (To report corporate misdeeds visit: ***www.sec. gov/whistleblower***.)

Not spotting problems can haunt a company for years. Even years after a company settles a federal investigation into wrongdoing, it can still face SEC fines if the agency uncovers faulty disclosures related to the earlier case.

Consider the long-running investigation of Mylan Labs and its expensive EpiPen treatment for severe allergy attacks. A multi-year investigation by U.S. Department of Justice into Mylan's inflated EpiPen sold to Medicaid resulted in the company agreeing to pay $465 million to settle the case.

In the fall of 2019, the SEC fined Mylan $30 million.

The reason? Incredibly, Mylan officials filed false and misleading statements in its disclosure of its last big penalty.

Nell Minow, an investor and shareholder activist, sees some improvement in corporate governance. But she still laments the lack of discipline in setting executive compensation. She tells business reporters writing about the CEO's pay to identify those responsible for writing the check – directors on the board's compensation committee.

"The great genius of the founding fathers was the idea of checks and balances as a fact of life," Minow said. "Checks and balances in the corporate world between shareholders, executives and the board are vitally important, yet we've had failure after failure after failure because of an imbalance of power."

Delaware Inc.

More than half of all U.S. public companies are incorporated in Delaware, regardless of their actual physical headquarters.

The state has a pro-business climate with fewer taxes and a "Chancery Court" that specializes in corporate lawsuits. A lone chancellor, not a jury, decides cases with speedy, written opinions that set precedent for future disputes across the country.

Leo E. Strine Jr. served as Chancellor of the Chancery Court and many of his rulings have reshaped U.S. securities laws and reduced plaintiffs' attorney lawsuits and fees. Yet relatively few have heard of the court unless they're with Wall Street law firms.

Indeed, the Chancery courtrooms in downtown Wilmington are eerily subdued, even during testimony. Lawyers from Wall Street law firms like Skadden Arps or Wachtell Lipton fill the first rows. A Bloomberg News reporter might be in the back row. When court adjourns, it looks like a fashion show for Ferragamo Balmoral shoes and Brioni suits as the attorneys exit to catch the Acela Express to Manhattan.

Strine worked in this haughty world, but is mindful of working-class realities, writing academic articles about aligning CEOs and worker interests back in 2006. He argues that American workers would be better off if all employees shared in the company's gains.

Strine echoes many of the themes of Franklin D. Roosevelt's "second bill of rights" speech in 1944. FDR believed Americans should have a secure job, a home, healthcare and retirement.

"I think what we lost sight of is the little guys," Strine said. "What we have in retirement or for our kids depends on our job. How much we are paid determines what we save."

This gulf between the "haves" and the "have nots" helped Trump get working and middle-class votes to win the 2016 race for the White House. It's a force seen in Britain as economic disparities fueled "Brexit," the nickname for a proposed exit from the European Union.

Unlike Trump, Strine actually respects business journalists who research issues, interview sources and "take it to a larger audience," he said. "People underestimate that translation role."

Strine laments how shrinking news staffs mean less coverage of important issues. Financial news is particularly vulnerable to quick-hit coverage on what's moving stocks each hour of the trading day. Just watch social media for blurbs that label events as black or white, good or bad.

"In business, gray is the predominant color," Strine said. The best business coverage should explain "how economic power affects lives of your society…what someone is doing to rivers and the air you breathe."

When asked to speak, he shares his personal ethics as a Christian and balancing them with the "harsh realities" of the criminal justice system. He cites the Golden Rule and Delaware's efforts to address prison overcrowding and inequities in punishment. Likewise, in analyzing giant corporations, Strine believes money managers, investors and journalists need to all think about deeper issues such as ethics and corporations' impact on consumers.

After serving on the Chancery, Strine was named to Delaware's Supreme Court and rose to be Chief Justice. Strine uses classroom lectures or guest speaking invitations to remind all to pay attention to Wall Street, especially the biggest institutional investment firms.

Consider what he calls the "Big Four" of Wall Street – BlackRock, Vanguard, State Street and Fidelity. The four funds are the biggest single owners of nearly 90 percent of the companies listed on the S&P 500 Index.

And get this: the fund managers shepherding billions of dollars in Americans' 401(k) retirement and 529 college savings accounts rarely even read corporations' SEC filings. If they did, they would get a clear picture of how management "accomplish favorable tax policy, extract subsidies for initiatives to grow" and favorable regulatory policies, Strine told one law school audience.

"Worker investors do not invest in mutual funds for political expression," said Strine, who stepped down from the court in late 2019. "They invest for retirement and college."

Corporate Filings Required By
the Securities and Exchange Commission

Name of Filing	What's in it?
S-1	Corporate registration statement, including the prospectus for newly-public companies.
8-K	Anything deemed "material," meaning the information could affect the company's financial performance. Includes information about appointments of new CEO, lawsuits, change in auditors.
10-Q	Company's quarterly financial statements.
10-K	Company's annual financial statements and report.
13-D	Must be filed by any outsider who buys five percent or more of the company's stock.
DEF-14A "Proxy" statement	Solicits shareholder votes on deals or election of board of directors. Reveals exec bios, employment contracts, pay, bonuses, shares held and stock options. Lists directors' pay and meeting attendance. Look for gems about use of corporate jets, houses and other perks. Lists largest shareholders and shareholder proposals.

Source: SEC.gov, Investigative Reporters & Editors Tip Sheets

9 | A Brave New Media World

The Federal Register chronicles the Byzantine tangle of 103 U.S. agency reports, ranging from endangered Gray Wolf updates to the annual White House proclamation of Leif Erikson Day. "It's a nightmare to search," said Francesco Marconi, the *Wall Street Journal's* research and development chief.

Marconi used AI, or artificial intelligence, to create an online tool to quickly sift through 200,000 unclassified documents for news, such as arms sales to Saudi Arabia. "This is transformative because it's accelerating work and making their lives easier," Marconi said. "We can do things that would have required months and dozens of people in a very short period of time." Innovation is in Marconi's blood – he's a fourth-generation descendent of Guglielmo Marconi, winner of the Nobel Prize for developing long-distance radio transmission.

Research and development work used to be limited to Merck drug labs and Duncan Hines test kitchens, not newsrooms. The *Journal* certainly didn't need it as the "Daily Diary of the American Dream" growing alongside Corporate America from the 1950s through 1990s.

"We were quasi-monopolies in a protected industry," said Matt Murray, *Journal* editor. "Now anyone can spread information and talk directly to people. There are no more interlocutors."

But the *Journal, New York Times,* and *Washington Post* are now investing millions in strategists like Marconi, software engineers and data scientists to speed up every aspect of journalism in the global sprint to win readers, subscribers and advertisers. The *Journal* added 36 new positions to staff innovation incubators in mid-2019.

The Big Three of U.S. news, meanwhile, are making strides to win back subscribers and advertisers to their core news business. Digital ad revenue did grow 23 percent in 2018, Pew noted, but half of the money went to Facebook and Google.

Meanwhile, loyal, Baby Boomer newspaper readers are aging. Millennials and Gen Z consumers rely on smart phones to orchestrate every move – ordering food, shopping for shoes and jeans, banking, posting photos and texting. Rarely do they use their mobile devices as an actual phone.

At the same time, readers of all ages are more accepting of the hybridization of news and sponsored content, such as multi-media "branded content" that brings in millions of dollars in revenue for the *Post* and *Times*. Private equity funds are investing in start-ups like Industry Dive in D.C. to produce industry-specific news and analysis.

Young business school entrepreneurs are launching chattier e-newsletters such at the *Morning Brew* and podcasts to reach millennials and Gen Z consumers who want quick, readable summaries of top business news, not their Dad's subscription to *Barron's* or *Forbes* magazines.

As future journalists and strategic communicators, it's important to understand the rapid changes that are happening as both the established "legacy" media companies and digital start-ups create new opportunities for your generation and beyond.

History books will show this era as a time when "mankind changed communications," said Emilio Garcia-Ruiz, one of the *Post's* managing editors.

More Engineers and a Cockroach Costume

Since Jeff Bezos, founder of Amazon, bought the *Post* for $250 million in 2013, he has pumped millions more into the news and business sides of the company. The *Post* now has about 900 journalists, up from 650 when Bezos took over.

Fred Ryan, *Post* publisher, said more engineers now work among journalists "to build things that are constantly improving on the product."

One of the biggest investments was building its own publishing software called Arc, which includes the core content management system, data analytics, video and advertising applications. The *Post* has since licensed the Arc package to other publishers. First came other newsrooms including the *Philadelphia Inquirer, Dallas Morning News* and Cox TV, among others.

In late 2019, the *Post* licensed Arc to BP, the giant oil company, which will use the software to publish newsletters and videos for its 70,000 employees. This is a potentially huge market given the size and growth of corporate communications departments, as well as outside PR agencies.

The *Post's* chief information officer, Shailesh Prakash, in 2017 estimated that Arc licensing could eventually produce $100 million in revenue for the *Post*, according to *Fortune* magazine.

The investment is paying off, but Ryan believes a far greater return is in "recruiting and retaining the best engineers. It's one thing to work for single company," Ryan said, but creating systems such as Arc has the "additional appeal of serving an entire industry."

One lingering challenge facing all news organizations is attracting and retaining younger readers to replace the aging Baby Boomers, a generation of loyal, daily newspaper readers. Focus groups, surveys, consultants and lots of committees have excavated the topic since the 1980s, but most of their studies are dust collectors on bookshelves.

The explosion of social media sites and other digital platforms forced the *Post* and others do a lot of experimenting on where to place news and ads. "We can put content where readers are," Garcia-Ruiz said. The *Post's* Snapchat edition has 2 million subscribers, mostly 14-to-22-year-old male users. If readers see it at a younger age, such as the *Washington Post* Discovery channel, "there's a better chance at age 28, you'll subscribe," he said.

For instance, the *Post* team started posting on TikTok, a mobile app that's a favorite of users aged as young as 11-years-old up to 30-somethings. They post 15-second videos of lip syncing, dancing or pranking friends. The app, known formerly as Musical.ly, was bought in 2017 by ByteDance, a privately-held start-up in China. Copycats have followed. Facebook's version is called Lasso.

Garcia-Ruiz relies on a team that mingles with teenagers and 20-somethings to see "something before our competitors and before me. We were on TikTok before I ever heard of it."

One reason that TikTok has grown with younger consumers is the light-hearted nature of the posts, including funny ones about serious issues. NBC News interviews with users showed like having a space to express themselves about climate change and politics. Said one: "I'm a teen and I would like to have fun. And talking about current issues with humor, to an extent, is a way for everything to seem less hopeless."

The *Post's* TikTok man is Dave Jorgenson, part of the creative video team, who can be found dressed as a giant cockroach for a quick climate change video or eating pumpkin spice-flavored Spam with his hands. But sometimes silly works. TikTok has about 16 million users, who spend about 46 minutes a day on the app. The *Post's* TikTok account hit 5.3 million views the week he gulped down the pumpkin Spam.

"Have we filled our core mission to serve democracy?" said Jeremy Gilbert, *Post's* director of strategic initiatives. "Probably not." But he adds that the *Post* has a history of public service journalism – breaking the Watergate scandal and publishing the Pentagon Papers in defiance of the White House – and lighter fare, such as the Style section.

Another multi-media project is developing the *Post's* intellectual property, about 300 daily articles, into television shows or documentaries. The short list of topics includes the Trump years, the Apollo space mission, scientology and opioids.

Some of the bigger newsroom projects, such as the 2019 series on the explosion of deadly opioids, are helping smaller news organizations, too. Journalists and data researchers created a massive database of opioid sales at pharmacies across the country, so local journalists could find data on nearby drug stores selling the most opioids.

"That's the work that we want to do and need to do," Grant said.

Meanwhile, the opioid epidemic was covered in "branded content" multi-media presentation created by a separate team of writers, videographers and designers at the *Post's* Brand Studio. That package was sponsored by Optum, a division of UnitedHealth.

To make sure that such content is never a conflict to the *Post's* strict policy of keeping advertising separate from the newsroom, all ideas must be cleared first with Executive Editor Marty Baron. And the content is labeled as being sponsored. "We do not deceive anyone," publisher Ryan said.

If there aren't "readers and advertising support, there won't be any journalism," Baron said. "We need to work with colleagues on business and engineering side and create products that are successful. At the heart of that business is the credibility of our journalism. That is something we can never forget. We don't have a business if we're not practicing credible journalism. We should never do anything that undermines the credibility of journalism."

> If there aren't "readers and advertising support, there won't be any journalism."
>
> —*Marty Baron*

The *Post* doesn't disclose sales from branded content but labeled it an "eight-figure business." That goes a long way in funding investigative journalism in newsrooms "and it means we're not chasing cute cat videos," Grant said.

Subscribers and traditional advertising still turn to the biggest and best news organizations, such as the *Times, Post* and *Journal*. One big reason: Readers seek out their expertise on major news, such as the investigations of Trump's business empire, tariff wars with China, climate change and detention of immigrants in border camps.

"We have benefitted from the change in the business model. People come to us to read the kind of stories the *New York Times* does best, not to read about the Kardashians," said Dean Baquet, *Times* executive editor. "People are willing to pay if it's something worth paying for. We have to go where they are and lose the notion that they'll eventually come to us."

Increased multi-media story telling has brought in a lot of readers. The *Times'* audience on YouTube has tripled in the past two years, said Nancy Donaldson Gauss, the *Times* executive editor of video.

One of the most ambitious projects at the *Times* is the "forensics investigative" team, which combines the traditional components – reporting, photos and video – with high-tech enhancements to help readers visualize what happened before, during and after news events. The *Times* has "so many varied skill sets," Gauss said. A former architect works in the newsroom to help recreate buildings in graphics.

The team uses Google Earth and geolocation to establish a common landmark to authenticate thousands of videos and photos gathered from eyewitnesses, satellite images, Facebook and other sources. For instance, five *Times* staffers spent about six months on a project to recreate two days of air strikes of Syrian hospitals to prove Russian pilots dropped the bombs.

The United Nations human rights' research showed that 50-plus healthcare locations have been attacked between April and October of 2019 in fighting over the Idlib Province. Russia has denied that its military was involved in attacking hospitals, which is a violation of international humanitarian laws.

But the *Times* obtained in-flight conversations between Russian fighter pilots and Syrian officials repeating "Srabotal" or "it's worked," after each bomb was dropped.

Another investigation pieced together the events leading up to the murder of journalist Jamal Khashoggi, a contributing columnist to the *Post.*

To do the story, the *Times* deployed more than 12 reporters, producers, researchers and visual journalists to show the case against his killers and the Crown Prince of Saudi Arabia, who U.S. and other investigators believe plotted the murder.

In addition to video and photos of the days leading up to the murder, the *Times* used FAA data to track planes and passports to show suspects arriving at the airport.

Another project reconstructed the massacre of 58 people at an outdoor concert by a shooter inside a Las Vegas hotel. The *Times* journalists pieced together seven days of video from the hotel and concert, maps and graphics. The visual story showed how easy it was for the gunman to get so many weapons into his hotel room, without being detected by security.

"Video is a powerful tool to engage a new audience," Gauss said. The demographics on YouTube viewers skews to a "different, younger audience which is exactly what we want."

Help Wanted: Openings for Business Journalists

Business news is enjoying a renaissance as entrepreneurs launch new digital sites and newsletters on corporate and Wall Street news, as well as obscure niches overlooked by the mainstream media.

Industry Dive, based in D.C.'s McPherson Square, was founded in 2012 by three investors with mostly business backgrounds, but light on journalism training. They pooled their savings and raised $400,000 from investors to start e-newsletters on a handful of topics.

Sean Griffey, CEO and co-founder, took an unconventional route to focus news coverage. He sees potential for broader audiences and revenue streams from highly-regulated industries, with tech disrupters and big capital spending budgets.

So far, that has translated into "dives" into 19 industries including electric utilities construction, solid waste and recycling, marketing and higher education. Some might view them as "unsexy, but they're not," Griffey said. "They affect everyone in this country."

Why target such an eclectic list? All of them have spiders' webs of suppliers, service providers and trade show planners. The target dive reader isn't the CEO of Duke Energy who is "not reading a lot of email newsletters," Griffey said. Their readers are "the next layer down."

The company hires journalists to write news and analysis because they bring legitimacy with the business readers "and the right to interact with them," Griffey said. When he started in 2012, the team had one reporter and freelancers. Now it has 70 journalists, with plans to hire about 20 more by the end of 2020. Most work in the D.C. office, but can set their own hours. The electric utility reporter works from home in the woods of upstate New York. "We're big believers on results-based culture. If the results are there, they can leave at noon."

The company's profits come from selling branded content and other ads, newsletter sponsorships, conference or trade show promotions. Advertisers can sponsor a series of five podcasts, for instance, for $47,500.

Industry Dive estimates its three-year growth rate at 348 percent in the fall of 2019. Griffey said the company has been profitable since early 2018 and has revenues of $30 million.

And the company caught the attention of some other big name investors: In September 2019, the partners sold a stake in the company to Falfurrias Capital Partners, a Charlotte private equity firm founded by former Bank of America CEO Hugh McColl Jr. and two others. All three founders remain in their same roles.

"We set out to build the next great media company," Griffey said, "and are still committed to doing that."

The Grandson of Business Journalism

American Inno is an example of new business models to sustain good journalism. The digital publication covers entrepreneurs and their innovations, which tend to get overlooked by bigger publications. It also sponsors events related to different industry niches so entrepreneurs can gather and hear from others in their fields. The company is part of American City Business Journals, a Charlotte-based publisher of digital and print business weeklies in 43 markets.

Inno started in Boston to cover tech start-ups and was acquired by ACBJ in 2015. It has expanded to 13 other cities, including Austin, D.C. and Chicago.

Unlike other start-ups, Inno won't enter a new city without outside funding. Generally, managers line up about $100,000 in economic development and business funds to launch and support the first year of publication. For instance, in Dallas, one of its partners is Thomson Reuters, which wants to invest in recruiting and retention of talented employees.

Its email newsletters offer news and deeper analysis on some topics most interesting to innovators. Most of it is original content, with some content coming from links to other publications. Some work for all markets is handled out of the Charlotte headquarters, with contract writers and full-time staff in select cities.

The staffs are so lean that Inno is experimenting with a new cost-sharing idea with its parent company. The *Tampa Business Journal* hired a second person to cover the tech beat, but the reporter will devote half of the work week to writing for Inno.

"We can't have folks just be journalists," said Geoff Shaw, president of Inno. "They have to be capable of writing and fostering community" at events. Shaw believes that "no one needs to hear from me. They want to hear from the voice in the newsletter every day. Events are content and programming."

In some ways, Inno shows the full circle of business journalism. Starting in the late 1970s, Geoff Shaw's grandfather Ray Shaw built ACBJ into a successful media company. Indeed, the company's growth was a big reason that metro newspapers beefed up their own business news coverage beginning in the 1980s.

Now the 38-year-old Shaw is part of the generation trying to find the right business model to sustain journalism in the 21st century. "We're not the Business Journals," Shaw said. But "we may learn a few things."

"Being in media now, whether you're on the journalist or business side, it's a challenging time," Shaw said. "There are a lot of broken models out there and folks have been slow to adapt."

In his R&D work, the *Journal's* research chief, Francesco Marconi, is also marking another full circle of the old and the new. To celebrate the 130th anniversary of the Dow Jones Industrial Average, his team set the DJIA's ups and downs from 1896 to 2019 to electronic music. The graphics department then produced a game called "Dow Cow," scoring an immediate 100,000 views from *WSJ* followers on Instagram.

ProPublica: Saving Local News

The Vindicator of Youngstown, Ohio is one of the few newspapers to get its own obituary.

Washington Post media critic Margaret Sullivan wrote it after visiting the Rust Belt community to talk to the family owners about shutting down the 150-year-old paper. Community members wiped away tears when they heard the news, but who could blame the "Vindy" owners? They looked for a buyer, but none made an offer for the paper, which had lost money in 20 of its last 22 years.

At its peak, the newspaper enjoyed profit margins of 17 percent, which Sullivan noted was just half what many metro newspapers made in the salad days of publishing before digital publications, Google and Amazon gobbled up the bulk of advertisements that used to fill newspaper pages.

Youngstown residents are used to bad news, recalling their version of "Black Monday" in 1977 when 5,000 neighbors were fired when Youngstown Sheet and Tube moth-balled the Campbell Works. Most recently, General Motors cut 1,400 jobs at its nearby plant.

Sullivan's column in the *Post* got a lot of attention as other media outlets did similar stories. A few days later, Youngstown got its white knight. ProPublica announced it would add a Youngstown reporter to its Local Reporting Network News project.

ProPublica is a non-profit, independent newsroom founded in 2007 by former *WSJ* managing editor Paul Steiger and newsroom attorney Dick Tofel. It has grown to 75 journalists and partnered with dozens of newsrooms to produce investigative reports. ProPublica has already won five Pulitzer Prizes.

Thanks to support from foundations and individual donations, ProPublica funded 20 other local partners in markets where newsroom cuts had crippled coverage of important issues.

"What's going on in Youngstown and the Mahoning Valley cries out for solid investigative reporting," said Stephen Engelberg, ProPublica's editor in chief. "We created the Local Reporting Network to fill that critically important need."

ProPublica can fund a Youngstown reporter's salary and benefits for a year, plus provide data and research, along with editing, design and other production help. The resulting stories will be published on various Ohio news sites, as well as ProPublica's website.

ProPublica and others know that there's no shortage of great stories that need to be told in Youngstown and around the globe. They're stepping in to fill some of the void left when traditional printed newspapers and magazines close shop. Its description of the newsroom's work is a reminder to all about the vital role journalists play:

"We dig deep into important issues, shining a light on abuses of power and betrayals of public trust – and we stick with those issues as long as it takes to hold power to account."

10 | Advice From the Pros: Be Curious, Concise and Caffeinated

Susanne Craig remembers her first day at the *Financial Post* in Toronto.

Her last job had been covering cops and city council at the *Windsor Star*, a daily newspaper in southern Ontario.

"I showed up and they said I was covering real estate companies. I didn't know what a publicly-traded company was and I had to cover earnings that day. I didn't know what net income was."

She turned to a colleague at the next desk, who was helpful and explained that "revenue is all the money that comes in and net is what's left over."

> "My message to young journalists: If you really want to be marketable and somebody who news organizations want, combine writing and reporting with a sense of the economy and how business works."
> —Dean Baquet

Craig learned the first step in a crucial part of any kind of reporting:

"If you're covering money, you need to understand how money is made," Craig said. "This is really important because it leads to other things."

Her boss at the *New York Times* agrees: "My message to young journalists: If you really want to be marketable and somebody who news organizations want, combine writing and reporting with a sense of the economy and how business works," said Dean Baquet, executive editor of the *New York Times.*

It served Craig well as she landed coveted jobs at two of the world's most prestigious newspapers: Covering Wall Street power brokers for the *Wall Street*

Journal and Donald Trump's business empire for the *Times*, where she is still digging into President Trump's tax returns.

Like the scores of journalists and communication professionals interviewed for this book, Craig offers some lessons learned that she wished she had known when she got started.

"Always read the fine print. At first, it can be intimidating, but just break it down into little pieces."

"Don't let people you cover intimidate you. They're just people."

Jason Zweig, The Intelligent Investor columnist at the *Journal* takes a slightly different approach to studying any financial documents.

> *"Whatever you're reading, pretend it's written in Arabic that goes from right to left. Start at end, read it back to front. Read the footnotes. The shit they don't want you to see is in the back. They put the glossy pictures in the front."*

Learn what the numbers mean in those financial statements and how to use them to tell stories. "Young people who are not afraid of numbers in stories are far more likely to get jobs," said Tracy Grant, one of the *Washington Post's* managing editors.

Being a journalist can be mentally and physically grueling work.

The *Washington Post's* David Fahrenthold advises journalists to "learn about yourself. What makes you a bad reporter?"

For him, he knows that if "I haven't had enough caffeine, I just don't care."

"But you have to be enthusiastic and energized to talk to strangers. It takes a lot of energy to do this. If you're tired, go home. You have to be physically present."

Fred Ryan, publisher of the *Washington Post*, believes that journalism's fundamentals – ethics, rigor, resolve to get to the facts, accuracy and objectivity – will endure. But "how it's delivered" will change at a quicker and quicker pace.

> *"The day they start as a rookie, until the day they retire as an experienced and wise person, things will be constantly changing. One thing we talk about a lot here is this culture of transformation. We will never be there. We will always be changing. Part of that is to*

have a culture of always being the challenger, never the incumbent. The challenger has got to be agile and has to deliver and win your vote. The incumbent relies on the past."

"A good editor can make you feel like you have the best job in the world," said Rachel Abrams, a *Times'* business reporter, who was part of the 2018 Pulitzer Prize-winning team that covered sexual harassment and misconduct in Hollywood. "A bad editor can ruin your life."

She encourages all to find allies and mentors, like she found in Sue Craig, who "is is never too busy to give me advice. That was invaluable."

"Being a journalist requires thick skin," she said, people who support you "make you grow into yourself." And show editors that you are tireless:

> *When you're just starting out, "say yes to every opportunity. Nothing is too small. You never know when you'll meet someone important. Build a network. Do as many stories as possible. Be really hungry and you'll go farther."*

And even when you're really tired, remember gratitude:

> *"Whether you're covering war, low-wage workers, Ford factory and sexual assaults by bosses or illegal immigration, it's important to remember it is a privilege to be paid to do what we do. When I'm feeling lazy, I tell myself: 'Nobody gets to do what I do.' Take it seriously."*

Lessons Learned From Strategic Communication Pros

Getting a communications job at a boutique agency or inside a Fortune 500 corporation requires that students learn many of the same skills as their friends who aspire to become journalists.

Indeed, some of the advice from both fields applies to any job, such as the need for thick skin, mentors, proper sleep and caffeine. To be sure, no one in the PR field suggested that they read documents backwards like the *Journal's* Zweig does in his job!

Communications veterans had a lot of detailed tips for students seeking a career in those fields, or for more experienced pros looking to make the next move. Here's what they had to say:

Stay up on the news by reading multiple sources, so you're current on economic and political trends that might affect your client. Becoming a good writer requires practice and attention to details. Proper grammar and spelling are essential, whether it's a quick email or a lengthy pitch to the CEO.

Don't trust spell check software because it doesn't catch everything, such as "their" instead of "there." This is a case where everyone should take Zweig's advice: Reading sentences backwards forces you to look at each word.

Proof every line for errors. Chris Turnbull, Carilion's head of corporate communications said:

> *"The most dangerous part of a communicator's job is missing a decimal point or a zero. Details matter."*

Concise and precise pitches require multiple edits. One New York PR vice president said:

> *"Read everything you write and cross out half the words."*

Learn the company and industry jargon, but don't expect your audience to decipher the meaning. Chet Wade, retired vice president of corporate communications at Dominion Energy laments "too many TLAs – three letter acronyms."

> *"Execs talk like that, but nobody understands that."*

Understand the financial statements, even if you do not write the quarterly earnings press releases. At some point, you might have to answer questions about lawsuits settlements, environmental fines or other matters that can result in special charges or gains to the company's results. You'll want to know how to gauge the financial impact if you're fielding questions from reporters, fellow employees or government officials.

Tailor the message for different audiences. Turnbull said:

> *"If you don't have a narrative to describe the financial topic, you will not reach your audience, unless it's a bunch of accountants."*

Learn the basics about journalism: Reporters have numerous deadlines for updating web stories, social media and stories for the next morning's edition. TV producers need visuals, not talking heads or documents. Learn when editors or producers have their news meetings so you know the right time of day to make your pitch.

Talk, don't just text, said one communications chief.

> *"Conversation skills have gone out the window. Meeting someone in real life means having a conversation, sharing a meal, talking about dogs and kids."*

Be curious, advised Turnbull.

> *"You have to be as good or better than the reporter at asking questions."*

Don't take it personally, advised one PR person in Manhattan.

> *"PR people get blamed for stuff that's beyond their control."*

(This might explain why several PR people interviewed didn't want to be named.)

Glossary of Terms

Buying on margin – The practice of putting very little cash down to buy a stock and using the actual stock as collateral for the rest of the purchase price.

Capital – Another name for money raised to invest in a business. It can also be used in "capital expenditures" or "CapX" which is money invested in plants or equipment for improvements.

Coincident indicators – Economic indicators that measure the current state of the economy, such as gross domestic product or personal income.

Collateralized Debt Obligations (CDOs) – Complex securities that hold various kinds of debt including bonds, car loans or mortgages. The bundle is then sliced into tranches and sold to investors. Each may offer different rates of return based on underlying risk. CDOs were used to repackage subprime mortgages which tanked after 2008.

Collateralized Mortgage Obligations (CMOs) – Loans that are bundled and sold to investors. CMOs are limited to holding mortgages.

C-Suite – All of the executive officers who are closest counselors of the chief executive officer, or CEO. They include CFO – chief financial officer, general counsel, or head attorney, COO – chief operating officer and CIO – chief information officer.

Dodd-Frank – The Dodd-Frank Wall Street Reform and Consumer Protection Act was passed in 2010 in response to the financial crisis of 2008. The law addressed problems in banking, mortgage lenders and credit-rating agencies.

The act established higher levels of reserves at banks and better disclosure of lending terms to consumers, among other changes. Many of the provisions were rolled back in 2018.

Dow Jones Industrial Average (DJIA) – Also called "the Dow," this started as a list of 12 company stocks in 1896. It has evolved over time to reflect changing industries and now has 30 stocks.

EBITA – Earnings before interest, taxes and amortization. Similarly, EBITDA tosses depreciation into what's excluded from the earnings measure. Some analysts and investors prefer this measure instead of net income because it strips away items to give a different picture of operations. Financial journalists use net income in earnings stories because EBITDA often paints a rosier picture of the company's financial health. Warren Buffett is suspicious of EBITDA because it could mean management "wishes to hide something."

Generally Accepted Accounting Principles (GAAP) – Adopted by the Financial Accounting and Standards Board (FASB) to create consistent rules governing which numbers are used for financial statements. GAAP numbers allow investors to compare one company to another. (See non-GAAP below.)

Glass-Steagall Act – Banking law that separated investment banking from consumer banks so depositors' money wasn't invested in risky stocks.

Gross Domestic Product (GDP) – Measure of U.S. economic activity, GDP is the value of all goods and services produced. The U.S. Bureau of Economic Analysis (BEA) lists GDP as the most popular indicator of the country's overall economic health.

Income – Also called earnings or profits. This is the money left after a company pays all its expenses.

Initial Public Offering (IPO) – The process of taking a private company to the public markets by issuing shares, or stock, in the company.

Insider Trading – Buying or selling a security on the basis of non-public information about the stock.

Junk bonds – Bonds that have a higher risk of default on the debt. They also carry a higher interest rate because of the risk. All bonds are rated based on risk. AAA bonds are the safest. Bonds rated BB or lower are considered junk.

Lagging indicator – An economic indicator that looks backwards to measure economic activities, such as the unemployment rate and corporate earnings reports.

Leading indicator – An economic measure that reflects what's ahead for the economy, such as housing starts.

Leveraged Buyout (LBO) – Buying another company with a large amount of borrowed funds. The assets of the company being bought are often used as collateral for the loans.

Material Information – Any information that could impact the value of a stock, and, if disclosed, could influence investors' decision to buy or sell the security.

New York Stock Exchange (NYSE) – The largest U.S. stock market and home to most prominent public companies. NYSE is often called the "Nigh-see" or "Big Board."

Non-GAAP – Figures that do not represent generally accepted accounting principles (GAAP) because they exclude one-time items, such as a loss related to restructuring. Sometimes called "adjusted" figures. The SEC allows companies to include non-GAAP figures in press releases, as long as it gives equal or greater space to the GAAP results.

Regulation Fair Disclosure (Reg FD) – The SEC passed this rule in 2000 to stop selective, advance disclosure of material information to a limited group of shareholders or market analysts. Reg FD requires that all shareholders and the public receive the same information simultaneously.

Sales – For most news stories, reporters use the term "sales" or "revenue" based on which work the company uses in press releases or financial filings. Sales are generated from whatever goods or services are sold to customers.

Sarbanes Oxley Act of 2002 (SOX) – Named for two sponsors in Congress, the law was passed in response to financial debacles at Enron, Tyco and

WorldCom. SOX tightened the rules on accounting, auditing and added criminal penalties for violations of securities laws. For instance, any corporate officer who signs off on inaccurate financial statements is subject to prison and other penalties.

Savings & Loan Associations – Nicknamed S&Ls or "thrifts," these institutions were established as a local alternative to big banks, especially for mortgages.

Securities and Exchange Commission (SEC) – U.S. government agency established by the Securities Act of 1934 to serve as the watchdog of public stock markets following the Great Crash of 1929.

Shares Outstanding – The number of shares of stock held by investors in a company. On balance sheets, shares outstanding are called "capital stock." Outstanding share totals each quarter should be compared to the year-earlier period. If the number of shares outstanding is higher or lower, check the footnotes to see if the company did a share buyback or issued new shares. Changes can boost or lower the earnings per share results.

Special Purpose Entities (SPEs) – A subsidiary created by a company to isolate a risky venture and protect the parent from financial harm. The SPE is often created to secure debt used in acquisitions or financing assets. The SPE is kept off the main company's balance sheet. In the case of Enron, SPEs were used to hide a lot of debt and toxic assets.

Stock options – Recipient has the right to buy or sell a stock at a certain price and date.

Subprime mortgages – real estate loan that charges a higher interest rate because borrower lacks the best credit report.

Ticker symbol – An abbreviation assigned to all publicly-traded companies. Ticker symbols were necessary when the actual ticker machine transmitted stock quotes on a thin strip of paper that couldn't accommodate full company names.

Sources: BEA.gov. Businessjournalism.org. Consumer Financial Protection Board. Corporatefinancialinstitute.com. Investopedia.com. Knowledge@Wharton. Morningstar.com. SEC.gov.

References

Chapter One

A Consumer Economy. Retrieved from ushistory.org

A&E Television Networks (2009) First stock ticker debuts. Retrieved from
www.history.com/this-day-in-history/first-stock-ticker-debuts

A&E Television Networks (2009) Great Depression: Hoovervilles. Retrieved from
https://www.history.com/topics/great-depression/hoovervilles

A&E Television Networks (2009) Great Depression: 1929 Stock Market Crash. Retrieved from
https://www.history.com/topics/great-depression/1929-stock-market-crash

A&E Television Networks (2009) U.S. Presidents: Franklin D. Roosevelt. Retrieved from
https://www.history.com/topics/us-presidents/franklin-d-roosevelt

A&E Television Networks (2009) President Gerald R. Ford. Retrieved from
https://www.history.com/topics/us-presidents/gerald-r-ford

A&E Television Networks (2009) Microsoft founded. Retrieved from
https://www.history.com/this-day-in-history/microsoft-founded

Bloomberg.com (2015) Drexel Burnham Oral History. Retrieved from
https://www.bloomberg.com/graphics/2015-drexel-burnham-oral-history/

Bradley, D. (2013, Oct. 18.) Former Johnson & Johnson PR Larry Foster, PR VP Dead at 88.
Retrieved from https://www.prweek.com/article/1274345/former-johnson-johnson-pr-vp-foster-dead-88

Cagan, M. (2016) *Stock Market 101: A Crash Course in Wall Street Investing*. Avon, MA: Adams
Media.

Coontz, S. (2018, April 10.) The Nostalgia Trap, *Harvard Business Review*.

Encyclopedia Britannica (2019) Charles Henry Dow, American Journalist. Retrieved from www.britannica.com/biography/Charles-Henry-Dow

Encyclopedia Britannica. Apple Inc. Retrieved from https://www.britannica.com/topic/Apple-Inc

Encyclopedia.com (2019) The 1960s Business and the Economy: Overview. Retrieved from https://www.encyclopedia.com/social-sciences/culture-magazines/1960s-business-and-economy-overview

Encyclopedia.com. 1980s Business and Economy. Retrieved from https://www.encyclopedia.com/social-sciences/culture-magazines/1980s-business-and-economy-topics-news

Federal Reserve. Savings and Loan crisis, Monetary Control Act of 1980, Garn St. Germain Act. Retrieved from https://www.federalreservehistory.org/essays/savings_and_loan_crisis https://www.federalreservehistory.org/essays/monetary_control_act_of_1980 https://www.federalreservehistory.org/essays/garn_st_germain_act

Federal Reserve. Stock Market Crash of 1987. Retrieved from https://www.federalreservehistory.org/essays/stock_market_crash_of_1987

Fortune (2012) How top executives live (Fortune, 1955). Retrieved from http://fortune.com/2012/05/06/how-top-executives-live-fortune-1955/

Foster, Lawrence G. (1999) Robert Wood Johnson - The Gentleman Rebel, State College, PA: Lillian Press.

Frankel, J. and Orszag, P.R. (2001, Nov. 2.) Retrospective on American Economic Policy in the 1990s, Brookings Institute.

Friedman, A. (2013, Oct. 18.) Lawrence Foster, who helped guide Johnson & Johnson through 'Tylenol cyanide crisis,' dies. Retrieved from https://www.nj.com/business/2013/10/lawrence_foster_who_helped_ste.html

Fundamentalfinance.com (2006) Stock Market Crash of 1929. Retrieved from http://stocks.fundamentalfinance.com/stock-market-crash-of-1929.php

Galbraith, K. (1954) *The Great Crash 1929*. New York: Houghton Mifflin Harcourt.

Hirsch, J. (2012) *The Little Book of Stock Market Cycles*. Hoboken, N.J.: John Wiley & Sons, Inc.

History of Business Journalism. Retrieved from http://www.bizjournalismhistory.org/main_frame.htm

Hoover, K. (2014, July 7.) Bull Market Began in Darkest Days of WW II. *Investors Business Daily.*

Interviews with Paul Steiger and Allan Sloan. Retrieved from http://www.bizjournalismhistory.org/frame_history.htm

Investopedia.com. Buying on Margin. Retrieved from https://www.investopedia.com/terms/b/buying-on-margin.asp

Investopedia.com. Hedge funds. Retrieved from https://www.investopedia.com/terms/h/hedgefund.asp

Investopedia.com. Leveraged buyouts. Retrieved from https://www.investopedia.com/terms/l/leveragedbuyout.asp

Investopedia.com. S&L Crisis. Retrieved from https://www.investopedia.com/terms/s/sl-crisis.asp

Investopedia.com (2010) Stock Then and Now: The 1950s and 1970s. Retrieved from https://www.investopedia.com/articles/stocks/09/stocks-1950s-1970s.asp

Johnson & Johnson. Former Johnson & Johnson PR Larry Foster, PR VP Dead at 88. Retrieved from https://www.jnj.com/our-company/former-johnson-johnson-corporate-vice-president-of-public-relations-lawrence-g-foster-dies-at-88

Kansas, D. (2005) *The Wall Street Journal Complete Money & Investing Guidebook*. New York: Crown.

Krugman, P. (2009, June 1.) Reagan Did It. The *New York Times*. Retrieved from https://www.nytimes.com/2009/06/01/opinion/01krugman.html

Lumen (2019) Conclusion. Post-war America. Retrieved from https://courses.lumenlearning.com/boundless-ushistory/chapter/conclusion-post-war-america/

Markham, J.W. (2006) *A Financial History of Modern U.S. Corporate Scandals: From Enron to Reform*. New York: Routledge.

Matthews, C. (2012, Oct. 22.) 25 Years Later: In the Crash of 1987, the Seeds of the Great Recession. *Time*. Retrieved from http://time.com/3741681/2000-dotcom-stock-bust/

Mauk, B. (2014, April 18.) The Ludlow Massacre Still Matters, *The New Yorker*.

McCartin, J.A. (2011, Aug. 2.) The Strike that Busted Unions, the *New York Times*.

McFadden, R.D. (2014, April 2.) Charles Keating obituary. The *New York Times*. Retrieved from https://www.nytimes.com/2014/04/02/business/charles-keating-key-figure-in-the-1980s-savings-and-loan-crisis-dies-at-90.html

Money.cnn.com (2004) Back to the '70s. Retrieved from https://money.cnn.com/2004/05/11/markets/seventies/

Money-zine.com (2019) Stock tickers and ticker symbols. Retrieved from www.money-zine.com/investing/stocks/stock-tickers-and-ticker-symbols

Murfson, S. (1999, March 10.) For R.J. Reynolds, A Topsy-Turvy History. Retrieved from https://www.washingtonpost.com/archive/business/1999/03/10/for-rj-reynolds-a-topsy-turvy-history/1c78c094-a345-429e-a627-95024dcfe55b/

Norris, F. (2012, Oct. 18.) A Computer Lesson Still Unlearned, the *New York Times*.

Original 12 stocks in DJIA (2018, June 20.) *Business Insider*.

Pavlik, J.V. and McIntosh, S. (2017) *Converging Media: A New Introduction to Mass Communication*. Oxford: Oxford University Press.

PR Academy (2014) Ivy Lee and the origins of the press release. Retrieved from https://pracademy.co.uk/insights/ivy-lee-and-the-origins-of-the-press-release/

Rehak, J. (2002, March 23.) Tylenol Made a Hero of Johnson & Johnson: The recall that started them all. Retrieved at https://www.nytimes.com/2002/03/23/your-money/IHT-tylenol-made-a-hero-of-johnson-johnson-the-recall-that-started.html

Ronald Reagan Presidential Library and Museum. Retrieved from https://www.reaganlibrary.gov/sreference/the-reagan-presidency.

Schmitt, J. (1999, Sept. 6.) Economic "Boom" of the 1990s is a Bust for the Middle Class, *Chicago Tribune*.

Scott, D.L. (2003) *Wall Street Words: An A to Z Guide to Investment Terms for Today's Investor*. New York: Houghton Mifflin Co.

Securities and Exchange Commission (2019) What We Do. Retrieved from https://www.sec.gov/Article/whatwedo.html#create

Stanford University (2005) Historical Trends in Executive Compensation 1936-2003. Retrieved from https://inequality.stanford.edu/sites/default/files/media/_media/pdf/Reference%20Media/Frydman%20and%20Saks_2005_Elites.pdf

Supreme Court Orders Standard Oil to Be Broken Up (2012, May 15.), the *New York Times*.

The Johnson & Johnson Tylenol Crisis. U.S. Department of Defense Joint Course in Communication. Retrieved from https://www.ou.edu/deptcomm/dodjcc/groups/02C2/Johnson%20&%20Johnson.htm

The Watergate Story. Retrieved from http://www.washingtonpost.com/wp-srv/politics/special/watergate/timeline.html

Thompson, S.A. and Power, W. (2017, Jan. 25.) The Ins and Outs of the Dow Jones Industrial Average, The *Wall Street Journal*.

Tylenol's Maker Shows How to Respond to Crisis. The *Washington Post*. p. WB1, October 11, 1982.

United Press International (UPI.) Year in Review: 1979. Business News. Retrieved from https://www.upi.com/Archives/Audio/Events-of-1979/1979-Business-News/

Chapter Two

Bloomberg, M. (1997) *Bloomberg on Bloomberg*, New York: John Wiley & Sons, Inc.

Investopedia.com. Company earnings announcements. Retrieved from https://www.investopedia.com/ask/answers/04/050604.asp

McKinsey.com. Avoiding the Consensus Earnings Trap. Retrieved from https://www.mckinsey.com/business-functions/strategy-and-corporate-finance/our-insights/avoiding-the-consensus-earnings-trap

Van Doorn, P. (2018, May 11.) Opinion: Why you can't trust Wall Street analysts. MarketWatch. Retrieved from https://www.marketwatch.com/story/why-you-cant-trust-wall-street-analysts-2018-05-08

Chapter Three

A&E Television Networks (2009) The Great Depression. Retrieved from https://www.history.com/topics/great-depression/1929-stock-market-crash

Barringer, F. (2002, Jan. 28.) Enron's Many Strands: Early Scrutiny, the *New York Times*. Retrieved at https://www.nytimes.com/2002/01/28/us/enron-s-many-strands-early-scrutiny-10-months-ago-questions-enron-came-went-with.html

CNBC.com. Warren Buffett Admits he Made a Mistake on Google. Retrieved from https://www.cnbc.com/2017/05/06/warren-buffett-admits-he-made-a-mistake-on-google.html

Egan, M. (2018, June 6.) Angelo Mozilo and his doomed mortgage machine. Retrieved from https://money.cnn.com/2018/06/06/news/companies/angelo-mozilo-countrywide-2008/index.html

Federal Reserve (2010) Ben Bernanke speech. Retrieved from https://www.federalreserve.gov/newsevents/speech/bernanke20100103a.htm

Inc.com. SEC disclosure rules. Retrieved from https://www.inc.com/encyclopedia/sec-disclosure-laws-and-regulations.html

Investopedia.com. CMO vs. CDO. Retrieved from https://www.investopedia.com/articles/investing/111213/cmo-vs-cdo-same-outside-different-inside.asp

Investopedia.com. Enron scandal summary. Retrieved from https://www.investopedia.com/updates/enron-scandal-summary/

Lerner, M. (2018, Oct. 4.) 10 Years later: How the housing market has changed since the crash. *Washington Post.* Retrieved from https://www.washingtonpost.com/news/business/wp/2018/10/04/feature/10-years-later-how-the-housing-market-has-changed-since-the-crash/?utm_term=.7e9bcf0f102d

Markham, J.W. (2006) *A Financial History of Modern U.S. Corporate Scandals: From Enron to Reform.* New York: Routledge.

Peters, J.W. and Romero, S. (2006, July 5.) Enron founder Dies Before Sentencing. Retrieved from https://www.nytimes.com/2006/07/05/business/05cnd-lay.html

Securities and Exchange Commission. Retrieved from https://www.sec.gov/litigation/complaints/comp18252.htm

Securities and Exchange Commission. Investor publications. Retrieved from https://www.sec.gov/reportspubs/investor-publications/investorpubsbegfinstmtguidehtm.html

Thebalance.com. Retrieved from https://www.thebalance.com/top-ten-economic-issues-in-2008-year-in-review-3305686

Thomas, C.W. (2002) The Rise and Fall of Enron. *Journal of Accountancy,* April. Retrieved from https://www.journalofaccountancy.com/issues/2002/apr/theriseandfallofenron.html

UPENN.edu (2018, Sept. 13.) The Real Causes and Casualties of the Housing Crisis. Retrieved from https://knowledge.wharton.upenn.edu/article/housing-bubble-real-causes/#

U.S. Senate Proceedings (2001, Dec.18.) Transcript of "An Overview of Enron Collapse." Hearing before the Committee on Commerce, Science and Transportation.

Wagner, S. and Dittmar, L. (2006, April.) The Unexpected Benefits of Sarbanes-Oxley. Retrieved from https://hbr.org/2006/04/the-unexpected-benefits-of-sarbanes-oxley

Yang, S. (2014, July 1.) 5 Years Ago Bernie Madoff Was Sentenced to 150 Years In Prison. Retrieved from https://www.businessinsider.com/how-bernie-madoffs-ponzi-scheme-worked-2014-7

Youtube.com. Diana Henriques "Ted Talk" on Bernie Madoff. Retrieved from https://www.youtube.com/watch?v=ijzgDYu1s9s

Chapter Four

Barrett, R. (2019, May 16.) Q&A: Whipsawed by low milk prices, more dairy farmers call it quits. *Milwaukee Journal Sentinel.* Retrieved from https://www.jsonline.com/story/news/special-reports/dairy-crisis/2019/05/16/whipsawed-low-milk-prices-more-wiconsin-dairy-farmers-call-quits/3304074002/

CNBC.com. U.S. China Trade War. Retrieved from https://www.cnbc.com/2019/08/07/us-china-trade-war-is-hurting-farmers-but-theyre-sticking-with-trump.html

Dummies.com. Analyst reports. Retrieved from https://www.dummies.com/personal-finance/investing/online-investing/how-to-access-analyst-reports-online/

Fitssmallbusiness.com. Retail analytics. Retrieved from https://fitsmallbusiness.com/retail-analytics/

Healy, J. (2009, Sept. 26.) Men's Underwear as an Economic Indicator, the *New York Times.* Retrieved from https://www.nytimes.com/2009/09/27/weekinreview/27healy.html

Investopedia.com. Comparable sales. Retrieved from https://www.investopedia.com/terms/c/comps.asp

Investopedia.com. Indicators and skirt length theory. Retrieved from https://www.investopedia.com/ask/answers/what-are-leading-lagging-and-coincident-indicators/ and https://www.investopedia.com/terms/s/skirtlengththeory.asp

Investopedia.com. Ratios. Retrieved from https://www.investopedia.com/ask/answers/05/lowperatiostocksbetterinvestments.asp

Moon, E. (2019, May 16.) The Fields are Washing Away Midwest, *Pacific Standard*. Retrieved from https://psmag.com/environment/the-fields-are-washing-away-midwest-flooding-is-wreaking-havoc-on-farmers

SeekingAlpha.com. Global grain markets. Retrieved from https://seekingalpha.com/article/4271749-corn-prices-move-supply-demand

Tyler, J. (2018, Aug. 22.) We visited a Walmart and a Target store, *Business Insider.* Retrieved from https://www.businessinsider.com/walmart-and-target-compared-pictures-details-2018-3

U.S. Department of Agriculture facts on China's agriculture imports. Retrieved from https://www.fas.usda.gov/regions/china

Vendhq.com. Key Performance Indicators. Retrieved from https://www.vendhq.com/images/university/retail-kpi-guide/Key_Performance_Indicators.pdf

Chapter Five

Bilton, R. (2016, Sept. 9.) How one *Washington Post* Reporter Uses Pen and Paper to Make his tracking of Trump get noticed. Nieman Lab.org. Retrieved from https://www.niemanlab.org/2016/09/how-one-washington-post-reporter-uses-pen-and-paper-to-make-his-tracking-of-trump-get-noticed/

Bogdanich, W. (2004, July 11.) In Deaths at Rail Crossings, Missing Evidence and Silence. Retrieved from https://www.nytimes.com/2004/07/11/national/11RAILS.html

Buettner, R., Craig, S. and Barstow, D. (2018, Oct. 2.) 11 Takeaways From the Times's Investigation Into Trump's Wealth, the *New York Times.* Retrieved from https://nytimes.com/2018/10/02/us/politics/donald-trump-wealth-fred-trump.html

Craig, S. (2002, May 10.) E*Trade Struggles, Shares Slip, But CEO Cotsakos is in Fat City, the *Wall Street Journal.* Retrieved from https://www.wsj.com/articles/SB1020977004641978840

Craig, S. and Hechinger, J. (2005, July 18.) A Wall Street Affair: This Bachelor Party Gets Lots of Attention, the *Wall Street Journal.* Retrieved from https://www.wsj.com/articles/SB1121649661535587999

Deutsch, C.H. (2000, March 26.) Private Sector: A Scholarly Shareholder Activist, the *New York Times*. Retrieved from https://www.nytimes.com/2000/03/26/business/private-sector-a-scholarly-shareholder-activist.html

Fahrenthold, D. (2016, Oct. 29.) Trump boasts about his philanthropy. But his giving falls short of his words, *The Washington Post*. Retrieved from https://www.washingtonpost.com/politics/trump-boasts-of-his-philanthropy-but-his-giving-falls-short-of-his-words/2016/10/29/b3c03106-9ac7-11e6-a0ed-ab0774c1eaa5_story.html

Fahrenthold, D. (2019, June 20.) When Trump Visits his Clubs, the *Washington Post.* Retrieved from https://www.washingtonpost.com/politics/when-trump-visits-his-clubs-government-agencies-and-republicans-pay-to-be-where-he-is/2019/06/20/a4c13c36-8ed0-11e9-adf3-f70f78c156e8_story.html?utm_term=.a0f4422f2846

Fahrenthold, D. (2019, July 10.) Nonprofit pulls out of strip club sponsored golf tournament at Trump club, The *Washington Post.* Retrieved from https://www.washingtonpost.com/politics/nonprofit-pulls-out-of-strip-club-sponsored-golf-tournament-at-trump-club/2019/07/10/d1fb8760-a352-11e9-b8c8-75dae2607e60_story.html?utm_term=.a8a3c87bffba

Fastenberg, D. (2010, Oct. 18.) Top 10 Worst Bosses, Time.com. Retrieved from http://content.time.com/time/specials/packages/article/0,28804,2025898_2025900_2026107,00.html

Investigatingpower.org. Interview with Walt Bogdanich. Retrieved from https://investigatingpower.org/walt-bogdanich/

McGeehan, P. (2003, Jan. 25.) Chairman Resigns from E*Trade, the *New York Times.* Retrieved from https://www.nytimes.com/2003/01/25/business/chairman-resigns-from-e-trade-his-big-pay-package-angered-investors.html

Millercenter.org. Roosevelt. Retrieved from https://millercenter.org/president/roosevelt/domestic-affairs

Sandomir, R. (2019, Feb. 5.) Albert J. Dunlap, Tough Executive Known as Chainsaw Al, Dies at 81, the *New York Times*. Retrieved from https://www.nytimes.com/2019/02/05/obituaries/al-dunlap-dead.html

Schacht, K. (2019, April 13.) The SEC's budget shows just how outgunned it is, *The Hill*. Retrieved from https://thehill.com/opinion/finance/438651-the-secs-budget-shows-just-how-outgunned-it-is

Whitehousehistory.org. State dinners. Retrieved from https://www.whitehousehistory.org/the-white-house-state-dinner

Chapter Six

Forbes.com. Public Relations. Retrieved from https://www.forbes.com/sites/robertwynne/2016/01/21/five-things-everyone-should-know-about-public-relations/#68ba84a02a2c

Garcia Cano, R. and Condon, B. (2019, July 31.) Trump 'rodent' tweets ring true at Kushner-owned Baltimore apartments, *Baltimore Sun.* Retrieved from https://www.baltimoresun.com/business/bs-bz-trump-kushner-baltimore-apartments-20190731-b7djej264nc67fdyp2zphhjnna-story.html

Heil, E. (2019, Sept. 12.) Now Popeyes is trolling America by inviting people to make their own chicken sandwiches, the *Washington Post.*

Isaac, M. (2019, May 10.) Uber's Stock disappoints, the *New York Times.* Retrieved from https://www.nytimes.com/2019/05/10/technology/uber-stock-price-ipo.html?action=click&module=RelatedCoverage&pgtype=Article&region=Footer

Kessler, G., Rizzo, S. and Kelly, M. (2019, Aug. 12.) President Trump has made 12,019 false or misleading claims over 928 days. Retrieved from https://www.washingtonpost.com/politics/2019/08/12/president-trump-has-made-false-or-misleading-claims-over-days/

Knowles, H. (2019, July 28.) Trump Attacked Baltimore. The city's newspaper wrote a scathing response. The *Washington Post.* Retrieved from https://www.washingtonpost.com/dc-md-va/2019/07/28/baltimore-sun-blasts-trump-attacks-city-better-have-few-rats-than-be-one/

Merriam-webster.com. Spin doctor. Retrieved from https://www.merriam-webster.com/words-at-play/word-history-spin-doctor#targetText=The%20effort%20of%20a%20spin,form%20of%20%22news%20management.%22&targetText=The%20name%20spin%20doctor%20became,presidential%20televised%20debates%20in%201984.

Modernmarketingpartners.com. Chiquita PR. Retrieved from https://www.modernmarketingpartners.com/chiquita-pr-campaign/

Rentz, C. and Reed, L. (2019, Aug. 15.) Volunteers picking up trash in West Baltimore save two men found overdosing. *Baltimore Sun.* Retrieved from https://www.baltimoresun.com/maryland/baltimore-city/bs-md-ci-overdose-20190815-20190815-vb7d6omdkvd35o4rt757xbyc3a-story.html

Rentz, C. (2019, Aug. 22.) One Baltimore woman wanted recycle bins for her public housing community, *Baltimore Sun.*

Ronson, J. (2015, Feb. 12.) How one stupid tweet ruined Justine Saccos life, the *New York Times.* Retrieved from https://www.nytimes.com/2015/02/15/magazine/how-one-stupid-tweet-ruined-justine-saccos-life.html

Stark, C. and Wiggins, O. (2019, Aug. 3.) Elijah Cummings defends Baltimore in wake of Trump's Twitter assault, the *Washington Post.* Retrieved from https://www.washingtonpost.com/local/md-politics/leader-of-md-democrats-blasts-gov-hogans-response-to-trumps-tweets-on-baltimore/2019/08/03/e07b30b8-b5f1-11e9-8f6c-7828e68cb15f_story.html

Sumagaysay, L. (2019, Aug. 22.) Uber faces another sexual harassment lawsuit from female engineer. *The Mercury News*. Retrieved from https://www.mercurynews.com/2019/08/22/uber-faces-another-sexual-harassment-lawsuit-from-female-engineer/

Taylor, K. (2019, Sept. 2.) Social-media battles, massive crowds, and overworked employees, *Business Insider.* Retrieved from https://www.businessinsider.com/popeyes-chicken-sandwich-rise-and-fall-story-2019-#targetText=Popeyes'%20new%20chicken%20sandwich%20set,it%20was%20officially%20sold%20out.

Wecanbemore.org. Recycling campaign. Retrieved from http://wecanbmore.org/wheelabrator-baltimore/

Yaffe-Bellany, D. and Sedacca, M. (2019, Aug. 29.) 15 Minutes to Mayhem: How a Tweet Led to a Shortage at Popeyes, the *New York Times*, Retrieved from www.nytimes.com/2019/08/29/business/popeyes-chicken-sandwich-shortage.html

Chapter Seven

Hirsch, J.S. (1991, Aug. 12.) Procter & Gamble Calls in the Law to Track News Leak, The *Wall Street Journal.*

New York Times (2003, May. 11.) Correcting the Record; Times Reporter Who Resigned Leaves Long Trail of Deception. Retrieved from https://www.nytimes.com/2003/05/11/us/correcting-the-record-times-reporter-who-resigned-leaves-long-trail-of-deception.html

Stern, G. (1991, Aug. 19.) Procter & Gamble Says Its Investigation of News Leaks Won't Lead to Prosecution, The *Wall Street Journal*.

Safire, W. (1991, Sept. 5.) Essay: At P&G, It Sinks, the *New York Times*. Retrieved from https://www.nytimes.com/1991/09/05/opinion/essay-at-p-g-it-sinks.html

Swasy, A. (1993) *Soap Opera: The Inside Story of Procter & Gamble.* New York: Times Books. *Wall Street Journal* (1991, Aug.13.) What Possessed P&G?

Chapter Eight

Bukszpan, D. (2015, Jan. 9.) Take note, Bob McDonnell, *Fortune*. Retrieved from https://fortune.com/2015/01/09/take-note-bob-mcdonnell-9-financial-criminals-who-made-good-after-prison/

CNBC.com. Elon Musk's tweets show that Tesla's board either can't or won't try to keep him in check. Retrieved from https://www.cnbc.com/2019/02/27/teslas-directors-seem-to-be-incapable-of-restraining-musk.html

CNN (2013, Oct. 24.) UK Phone hacking scandal fast facts. Retrieved from https://www.cnn.com/2013/10/24/world/europe/uk-phone-hacking-scandal-fast-facts/index.html

Corporatefinanceinstitute.com. Front running definition. Retrieved from https://corporatefinanceinstitute.com/resources/knowledge/trading-investing/front-running/

Delaware.gov. Corporations and Chancery history. Retrieved from https://corpfiles.delaware.gov/whycorporations_web.pdf and https://courts.delaware.gov/chancery/history.aspx

Investopedia.com. Delaware as tax shelter. Retrieved from https://www.investopedia.com/articles/personal-finance/092515/4-reasons-why-delaware-considered-tax-shelter.asp

Kolhatkar, S. (2019, April 8.) The SEC Takes on Elon Musk's Tweeting, Again. Retrieved from https://www.newyorker.com/business/currency/the-sec-takes-on-elon-musks-tweeting-again

New York Times (1988, Feb. 27.) Broker in Winans Case is Sentenced. Retrieved from https://www.nytimes.com/1988/02/27/business/broker-in-winans-case-is-sentenced.html

Perez-Pena, R. (2007, Dec. 14.) News Corp. Completes Takeover of Dow Jones, the *New York Times*. Retrieved from https://www.nytimes.com/2007/12/14/business/media/14dow.html

Pierson, B. (2019, April 26.) Tesla's Musk agrees to new vetting rules for tweets in SEC deal, Reuters. Retrieved from https://www.reuters.com/article/us-tesla-musk-sec/teslas-musk-agrees-to-new-vetting-rules-for-tweets-in-sec-deal-idUSKCN1S22BV

Rapier, G. and Matousek, M. (2019, Sept. 19.) Tesla: Key names who have departed in the past year, *Business Insider*. Retrieved from https://www.businessinsider.com/tesla-executive-departures-list-2018-9

Reuters (2012, April 3.) Timeline: News Corp. and the phone-hacking scandal. Retrieved from https://www.reuters.com/article/us-bskyb-murdoch-newscorp/timeline-news-corp-and-the-phone-hacking-scandal-idUSBRE8320MQ20120403

SEC.gov. Retrieved from https://www.sec.gov/news/speech/2014-spch062314mjw and https://www.sec.gov/news/press-release/2019-42

Winans, R.F. (2011, Aug. 16.) SEC Declares Educated Guessing Illegal, *Business Insider*. Retrieved from https://www.businessinsider.com/sec-declares-educated-guessing-illegal-2011-8

Chapter Nine

Beaujon, A. (2019, June 19.) There Is, in Fact, a Plan, the *Washington Post*. Retrieved from https://www.washingtonian.com/2019/06/19/there-is-in-fact-a-plan-behind-the-washington-posts-gloriously-weird-tiktok/

Digiday.com. Branded content. Retrieved from https://digiday.com/media/branded-content-margin-pressure-squeezes-publishers/

Digiday.com. Deep fakes. Retrieved from https://digiday.com/media/the-wall-street-journal-has-21-people-detecting-deepfakes/

Federal Register documents. Retrieved from https://www.federalregister.gov/

Ingram, M. (2017, March 13.) How the *Washington Post* Makes Money From its Competitors. Retrieved from https://fortune.com/2017/03/13/washington-post-arc/

Marshall, J. (2016, Dec. 11.) Publishers take on Ad-Agency Roles, the *Wall Street Journal*. Retrieved from https://www.wsj.com/articles/publishers-take-on-ad-agency-roles-with-branded-content-1481457605

Pewresearch.org. U.S. newsroom facts. Retrieved from https://www.pewresearch.org/fact-tank/2019/07/09/u-s-newsroom-employment-has-dropped-by-a-quarter-since-2008/ and https://www.pewresearch.org/fact-tank/2019/07/23/key-takeaways-state-of-the-news-media-2018/

Poynter.org. TikTok at *Post*. Retrieved from https://www.poynter.org/reporting-editing/2019/how-the-washington-posts-tiktok-guy-dave-jorgenson-gets-millions-of-views-by-being-uncool/

Rosenblatt, K. (2019, Jan. 11.) What is TikTok? Retrieved from https://www.nbcnews.com/tech/internet/what-tiktok-how-short-form-video-app-took-over-internet-n956751

Sullivan, M. (2019, July 7.) Democracy is about to die in Youngstown, the *Washington Post*. Retrieved from https://www.washingtonpost.com/lifestyle/style/democracy--is-about-to-die-in-youngstown-with-closing-of-the-local-newspaper/2019/07/05/e428e26a-9da4-11e9-b27f-ed2942f73d70_story.html?utm_term=.c373b6adabd7

Wall Street Journal (2019, March 6.) Compare any two Colleges. Retrieved from https://www.wsj.com/articles/compare-any-two-colleges-from-the-wsj-the-college-rankings-11551886824

Chapter 10

Brands, H.W. (2010) *The First American: The Life and Times of Benjamin Franklin,* New York: Knopf Doubleday Publishing Group.

Acknowledgments

Frank Allen, the *Wall Street Journal's* Philadelphia bureau chief, visited a Penn State Journalism class in 1983 to talk about the newspaper's legendary page-one features. By the end of his humorous lecture, I knew that I wanted to work for him.

I got my chance during a summer internship. But feature writing is the brownie-after-you-eat-your-broccoli. First, I had to learn how to cover publicly-held companies on the spot news desk.

Thank goodness Frank had hired a few other patient journalists willing to help the intern. They taught me a lot about deciphering obtuse press releases and financial statements. After a few weeks, I got my chance to write my first *Journal* feature – a story about a fisherman catching eels from a flimsy skiff on the choppy Chesapeake Bay. His daily catch landed on the plate of a swanky D.C. restaurant plate, where I learned eel is tasty if disguised with beurre blanc.

My internship led to a full-time reporting job and many adventures at the *Journal*. I wrote a lot of critter features – the trendy brown bats in suburbia, bloody cockfights in Kentucky and emus in Amish country. Plus, an eel sequel about a Florida potato farmer who gave up spuds to raise young eels to sell to European connoisseurs.

My corporate beat was Procter & Gamble Co., the Cincinnati-based maker of detergents, shampoo and toothpaste. Sounds boring, but I found some good stories following soap salespeople in Lima, Peru and a garbologist who studies the lifespan of Pampers diapers in Arizona landfills. And I learned from P&G's bully tactics how far a big company will go to make money.

Looking back, I now realize that first summer on the spot news desk in Philly would've been a lot easier if I had a book about business reporting. That's why I wrote this book – to help a new generation of Journalism and Strategic Communication students learn how to understand, then weave financial data into their work. Whether they go on to careers as journalists or PR people, having the skills to write well and decipher financial information makes them more competitive in the digital marketplace.

Besides Frank, I've been fortunate to adopt other mentors on my path from newsrooms to classrooms. Dean and Sue Mills, my "adopted parents" since my days at Penn State, have cheered me on for 37 years. Dean is a terrific mentor and editor of this and my three previous books. And trust me: His eye and pencil seem to grow sharper each time!

I relied on other friends to read the manuscript. Many thanks to Lynn Holley for her insights about business reporting and crisis communications. She worked in both fields, making her a dream interview and editor for the project. And I'm grateful to Tom Contiliano at Bloomberg News for his tutorials on financial statements and metrics. Tom is a terrific visiting professor who has helped scores of students and journalists decipher financial data.

Learning more about the Strategic Communication field introduced me to some fantastic pros, including Dave Curley, Chris Turnbull and Chet Wade. They were incredibly generous with their time and provided valuable examples and tips to enrich the book.

Academic and journalism colleagues brainstormed ideas and offered feedback as well. Special thanks to Mizzou friends Martha Pickens and Suzette Heiman for their assistance. Mizzou is fortunate to have a fine Business Journalism program led by Randy Smith, a fellow Reynolds Chair. As another journalist-turned-professor, Randy helped brainstorm early ideas for a textbook. I'm grateful for his counsel and friendship.

One of the gifts of researching a practical textbook is visiting with so many terrific and hard-working journalists. The book is greatly enriched by the insights from interviews at Bloomberg News, Industry Dives, the Morning Brew, the *New York Times*, ProPublica, the *Wall Street Journal,* and the *Washington Post,* among others.

I'm especially grateful to Sue Craig at the *Times*. Sue is a tireless and tenacious reporter who accomplished something that even Congress can't do: She got a decade of President Trump's tax returns. Her continued work is a lesson on the importance of following the money and holding powerful people accountable to the public. Despite her busy schedule, Sue was kind to provide feedback and support.

Former Journal colleagues including editor Matt Murray and Paul Steiger reminded me how much I learned from my *Journal* years. A visit with Paul also reminded me how much he supported me when CEOs and PR people whined about my coverage.

At the *Post*, Marty Baron, Tracy Grant, Emilio Garcia-Ruiz, David Fahrenthold and Fred Ryan shared stories and tips to give the perspective at intersection of power, money and politics.

Getting a book across the finish line requires a lot of help from the publisher. Thanks to Felisa Salvago-Keyes and Grant Schatzman at Routledge. My friend Jenny Young shared her time and talents to design the book. Thanks to Robert Trigaux and Sarah Bartlett for reading the proof pages just one more time.

Interviews, travel and all the other details of doing a book rely on the generosity of people who provide financial support to authors. I'm especially indebted to the Donald W. Reynolds Journalism Institute for providing research funds, starting as a graduate student at the Missouri School of Journalism from 2009 to 2014. Now I'm privileged to hold one of the four Reynolds Chairs at the nation's finest Journalism programs. Beyond research support, the Reynolds endowment funds business journalism internships to prepare our students for great jobs at American City Business Journals, Bloomberg News, the *Washington Post,* and the *Wall Street Journal*, among others.

At Washington & Lee University, we are fortunate to receive summer Lenfest Research Grants. Thanks to W&L Provost Marc Conner for supporting my work with that grant and other publication funds. And thanks to my Journalism & Mass Communication department colleagues and my students for their encouragement throughout the project.

It's been said that a friend is someone who lets you think out loud. Thankfully, I have a big circle of patient listeners. I'm grateful for the wisdom and laughter from Lynne Anderson, Aly and Shelia Colon, Kevin Finch, Lindsey Nair, Stephanie Sandberg, Louise Uffelman, Stephanie and Matt Veto, among others. You sustain me whether near or far away.

Most of all, I offer my thanks to my extended family who cheer me on with their humor and love. This book is dedicated to my mother Maribel Allison Swasy, who worked alongside John, my farmer father, tending to eight children and feeding a cast of field hands. When the household budget was tight, she worked nights as a nurse to make extra money. She nurtured my love of reading and writing by always buying me a boxload of books, notebooks and pens for me to find that next good story.

Index